A Walk Through Time

Gary Fowler

Order this book online at www.trafford.com
or email orders@trafford.com

Most Trafford titles are also available at major online book retailers.

Print information available on the last page.

ISBN: 978-1-4122-0213-8 (sc)
ISBN: 978-1-4120-9577-8 (hc)
ISBN: 978-1-4251-9401-7 (e)

Trafford rev. 12/23/2019

www.trafford.com
North America & international
toll-free: 1 888 232 4444 (USA & Canada)
fax: 812 355 4082

Acknowledgments

A person's life is seldom told perfectly by the way he or she remembers it. Because of human error and forgetfulness, the memories I recall may not always be completely accurate with the way events actually occurred; but they are my memories nonetheless.

I am so very grateful for all the generous help I received from Mrs. Renee Nelson who spent many hours correcting my writing and spelling. She reminds me of Shirley Temple with all her red hair, her enormous smile, and her willingness to help other people. Thanks Renee! The world needs more people like you.

I wrote these memoirs because my mother asked me to. I know Mom, you always wanted the best for all your children, and I love you and thank you for all the love you shared with me. You told me I could do anything I set my mind to, so I set my mind to do this for you. Here are the things  I remember best.

Love You
Gary

Table of Contents

Two Much

To Gary Fowler
with best wishes   Geo Bush.

The number two has played a very important part in my life and has even guided some of my future destinies into eternity. I have bought two houses, two new boats, two new cars, and have been married twice. I have wanted two children and aborted two, which I am doubly sorry for. Thinking I was smart, I became stupid which makes two states of mind. I have one child which the Lord was gracious enough to give me, but my second wife wouldn't have the second child we had agreed on before getting married, a positive changing into a negative, to my dismay. So I have learned that people can change destiny. Christ, who came to earth as a man, gave me a second life—another two for me.

Good and evil make up life as we know it and without the two, heaven and hell would be set apart as God has planned it and it will prevail.

My two careers, military and civilian, have lasted over twenty—two years each, and most of the decisions in my life could have taken two courses, either good or bad, sometimes both. I have loved twice and divorced twice which was both good and bad. Night and day are also present in the two of things, like black and white, cold and hot, and rich and poor, which are ever present in this double standard world we live in, which is either coming or going. I have also known two President Bushes, one I liked and voted for and the other I didn't like and didn't vote for. Are those two more things to consider? Should I go on or stop here? Will that make you happy or sad? Maybe I am just thinking too much.

This is April, my daughter, and her husband Sean with the pilot of a Bi-Plane hangared at St. Mary's Airport. They were taking aerial pictures for me that day.

Accounting

Accounting for one's self can be a job that is never finished. Accounting for one's resources will always leave you wondering. And studying accounting will provide you assets, while you count your debits, and manage your credits.

Tell

When I was very little, I embarrassed my Mother while we were shopping by a Hagerstown department store.

Show

Once when I was very little, I embarrassed my Mother while she was looking in a department store window in Hagerstown. When she turned around, she saw me peeing in the gutter on Main Street. People were walking by and looking at me, so she kept on looking in the store window. When I had finished, I walked over and stood beside her. She didn't look up, she just took my hand and we walked away.

A Frog Tale

My  First Memory Of An Animal.

        I guess I was around four years old and living on a farm near Greencastle, Pennsylvania. We had no electricity, and so no electric cooler or refrigerator. The year was around 1946. The first electricity I can remember was a light put in over the outhouse, two holes without the moon on the door, which made going to the bathroom in the middle of the night a lot better for a little boy like me.

        Anyway, we had a spring house where the milk was cooled after milking the cows and while waiting on the milkman to come to pick it up for bottling and then deliveries. And in this spring house, besides other things, lived a big green frog. I would try my best to be quiet and sneak up on this creature, but just as soon as I would get close to him he would jump into the spring well, and down to the bottom he would go. The water was very cold and deep, but there was nowhere for him to hide, so he would just sit there and look up at me.

However, the water was too deep for a little boy like me, and the way he looked at me, I could tell he knew it. I never did catch that big green frog, and to this day I wonder what ever happened to him.

This was one of my favorite pets.
When I got older I called
her "Momma Kitty."

First Technology I Can Remember

Putting an electric light over our outhouse was the first real technology advancement I can remember. After that, it was the radio which we all loved to listen to, especially programs like," The Shadow Knows" and "Amos'n Andy." The automobile was probably there before the electric light, but I remember electricity first because of the advantages it provided me—like not getting bit by a snake or having something come out of the two holes and eating me while I used the dreaded outhouse at night. We didn't have plastic pools back then either. As a matter of fact, my bathtub was a metal basin with water heated from a wood burning indoor stove. Chilly at first, but a big fluffy towel warmed me right up.

Aunt Pancake

After my biological father left my mother and me, Mom took me to live with Aunt Frances awhile, until she could get settled and on her feet. Aunt Frances lived on Rock Cliff Drive near Martinsburg, West Virginia in the country. She was married to Richard Small who worked as an accountant for the railroad in Martinsburg. I remember he used to come home from work sometimes with a half gallon of ice cream, strawberry seemed to be the favorite, and we would eat it on the back porch. If the Homer boys were coming up the road though, we went inside; I was told that unless I wanted to share my ice cream with them I had to eat it inside. I played with the Homer boys sometimes; they lived one house down the road about a quarter of a mile. But Aunt Frances didn't give me much ice cream, and we didn't have it that often, so I didn't want to share it with them. I can't remember their names, but I do remember that their family was a lot poorer than ours. It didn't make any difference to me, I still didn't want to share my strawberry ice cream with the two boys; there just wasn't enough to go around.

I used to call Aunt Frances "Aunt Pancake" because she made pancakes in the morning for me. And when I had a cold or a fever she made a hot toddy for me with sugar, whiskey, (4 Roses) and water. I remember sweating in the bed most of the night under heavy quilts that smelled of mothballs, but in the morning my fever would be gone. She would make my favorite breakfast of pancakes, and afterwards she rocked me in a hickory rocker that I still have in my house today.

I can remember a lot from when I lived on Rock Cliff Drive. Like when they made chicken salad, for example. Uncle Richard used to chop the heads off of five or six chickens and let them flop around on the ground until they were dead, with blood flying everywhere. But Aunt Frances showed me that if you made a cross on the ground, then cut the head off of a chicken and laid it upside down on its back on top of the cross, it would not move off that spot. I never knew why the chicken didn't move, but I saw her do it and it worked. She also told me that if I could guess who was thinking about me my hiccups would stop. That seemed to work sometimes; the other times I guess I just couldn't guess who was thinking about me. Anyway, after the chickens were dead, she scalded them in boiling water, and then picked the feathers off them. I used to hate the smell of hot wet chicken feathers. Aunt Frances would then take out the insides of the chickens, sometimes finding a soft egg which had not been laid yet. All this usually made a washtub full of chicken salad. She froze some and refrigerated the rest.

Uncle Richard not only raised chickens but he also had a small garden and I used to help him plant potatoes, snap beans, corn, radishes, lettuce, carrots, onions, cantaloupe, rhubarb, squash, peas and pumpkins. Aunt Frances planted flowers at the very

12

end of the garden and around the house. Her favorite flowers were violets and cactus which she kept inside the house. I can remember in the evening at harvest time sitting on the back porch with Aunt Frances, swinging on a two seat swing, snapping beans and husking corn for canning.

One evening when we came back from Martinsburg, after stopping at a Tastee Freez for some soft ice cream, there was a copperhead snake under the swing and Uncle Richard killed it with a hoe. The porch had a tin roof over it and I loved to swing on the swing, listen to the rain hit the roof, and watch the lightning flash. Under the porch was a cistern full of rain water which came off the tin roof of the house and down the drain pipe. There was a hand pump mounted over the cistern that we used to get water for washing clothes and cleaning up. Uncle Richard had to clean out the cistern every once in awhile when it got full of leaves and sludge.

There was a peach tree right next to the porch that I remember for two reasons. Sometimes when I did something I wasn't supposed to do, like going up over the hill by a billboard where hobos sometimes went to drink their whiskey, I needed a whipping. Aunt Frances used to make me go get a switch off the peach tree and after telling me it was going to hurt her more than me, she placed three or four welts on my back side and/or the back of my legs as I tried to get away. The peaches on the tree also made for some delicious pies.

I also recall going hunting for mushrooms. They showed me which mushrooms were safe to eat and which mushrooms were poisonous. I learned a lot of things from my Aunt and Uncle. I remember Uncle Richard telling me that rocks don't start to come out of the tread of your car tires until you travel fifty-five miles per hour or better.

Aunt Frances never had any children of her own and when Mom came to take me back one day, they got into a fist fight. Mom knocked Aunt Frances backwards and her foot got caught in a wash bucket. Aunt Frances didn't want Mom to take me, which was the reason for the fight, but Mom won and we left for Hagerstown, Maryland.

Both Aunt Frances and Uncle Richard have since passed away. Aunt Frances died when I was in the Air Force and stationed at Anderson Air force Base, Guam. She was working for The White House Apple Company picking apples when she had her heart attack. Uncle Richard died of cancer in the Martinsburg Hospital many years later; I did get to hold his hand before he departed for his heavenly home and I have his daily diary which he kept most of his adult life. When his wife, Frances passed away, his entry was "I'll see you later little darling." I will always remember them with love and affection.

Ghosts

I remember while staying at the Barnhart's in Greencastle, Pennsylvania, there was a man who everyone called Uncle Jake. I don't know if he was some relation to the Barnharts or if that was just an affectionate name they gave him. He didn't have much; matter of fact, I used to see him sitting on the steps of the Barnhart's porch sharpening his razor blades on a half round piece of glass because he didn't have the money to buy new ones. He lived at the end of the meadow near the Barnhart's farm in an old wooden house that had never been painted. Mom Barnhart used to send one of her daughters to fetch him for dinner sometimes and I would go along. We would follow a small creek down the meadow and around a hill which had woods on it. The meadow opened into a valley, and there was a small pond on the other side of a road that ran between the meadow and his old house. It was a pretty long walk for a little kid, but I enjoyed looking for frogs, fish, and turtles in the water of the creek. I was afraid of the cows that were sometimes in the meadow and was glad that Patsy or Barbra Ann Barnhart was there with me. I sometimes saw a snake around the creek, and I had to watch where I stepped because of the cow

15

droppings in the meadow. Patsy or Barbra Ann would get mad if I stepped in one. But it was only the fresh ones you had to worry about; the other ones got so hard that I could throw them and skip them across the water. I guess that is why I had to wash my hands before I ate. I wondered how they knew I was skipping cow pods.

Uncle Jake told me a ghost story one time and I still tell it to the kids when I get a chance. It goes like this: Once upon a time, not far from here, there was an old house that some people say was haunted. Nobody knows what happened in this house, but people believed there were two children, a boy and a girl, about your age, that had died in the bathroom upstairs. And on some nights, like this one, you could hear coming from the upstairs bathroom in a low whispery voice, "It flo-o-o-ats, it flo-o-o-ats." Now there was a man who had a son named Peter and a daughter named Mary. And wherever Peter went, his younger sister would go because they were very close. But one evening Mary was sent to the store to buy some milk, which they needed for cereal in the morning before school, and Peter was busy helping his father fix the sink in the kitchen. Mary decided to take a shortcut through a field near their house which took her past this old house, but she didn't know it was haunted. As she crossed onto the road from the field and got by the gate leading into the house she noticed a dim light in the upstairs window, and carried by a faint breeze she heard, "It flo-o-o-ats, it flo-o-o-ats". She then ran all the way to the store, and after taking the long way home, she told her father and brother what had happened. Her father knew the stories about the house and told both children to stay away from it and never go there again, even though he believed it was only the wind that Mary had heard.

The next day Mary talked to her brother and asked if he believed her. Peter was a very brave boy and since he cared for his sister and wanted to believe her, he said, "Let's go and see what you heard." The moon was full and bright but the clouds covered it occasionally, making it a lot darker at times. When Peter and Mary arrived at the gate, the moon lit the house and all the grounds around it, giving it a shadowy look, especially near the small graveyard along the side of the property. As Peter opened the gate he could tell it had not been opened in awhile, because it sque-e-e-aked as it came to a stop about halfway. Peter started in, with his sister right behind him; still they heard no sounds. When they got to the steps leading up to the front door, they noticed one of the four steps was missing, but still they heard no sound. They were careful to step over the missing step, just as the clouds went in front of the moon, making it darker and almost black on the covered porch as they approached the door leading into the house. It was already open about three inches, so Peter pushed it all the way open. They heard it sque-e-e-ak, but there was no other sound. The moon had come out again, and they could see a staircase leading upstairs, a large open room to their left, and two small doors to their right. When they went in and started up the stairs they heard a sque-e-e-e-king door open and they saw a dim light at the top of the stairs. The door leading into the house slammed shut, **BAM**! Then they heard a whispery voice saying, "It flo-o-o-ats, it flo-o-o-ats." Mary almost fell down the stairs, but Peter, being braver, said,

*"What Floats?" And then they both heard, "Ivory Soap Floats."
The End!*

*This is Mom Barnhart and her
two daughters, Barber Ann and Patsy.*

As A Child

As a child I was alone. It was not my choice, but destiny that set my course. I was abandoned by my father whose idea of freedom didn't include a son. My mother, who loved me, was kept busy providing a home for my sister, Paulette, and me. And my peers, like a lot of children, were either bullies who wanted to make themselves feel more important, or just plain greedy for what they could get. And of course there were the nerds who knew everything or whose families were more important than the general populous. I survived by running away from or outsmarting these developmental playmates. I was very insecure and non-trusting of people trying to help me, which made me more of a loner. I learned to get along with others, but that was their world not mine.

I used to go to sleep at night with my head under my covers to protect me from a clock in my room that I remember getting louder and louder, **tick tock Tick Tock TICK TOCK.** After a while it would start to fly, in my mind, and spin around the top of the room, getting faster and faster like a speeding bullet squaring the corners as it went around the ceiling. I hid under the covers so it would not hit me. I know now that this was all in my mind, but when I was a child it was very real.

At the schools I attended—one or two a year because we moved a lot—I felt they wanted to either punish or expel me, so I did what I had to do, but I wasn't motivated. I quit doing the homework because I didn't understand it and I wasn't motivated at all in that direction. Besides, the teachers seemed to have their favorites, and I wasn't one of them. This is what I remember from childhood. The teachers always had suggestions for my mother, when she could make the P.T.A. meetings, but she was mostly working overtime to put food on the table. They would tell her, "He needs to pay more attention, and he hardly ever does his homework, but he doesn't misbehave in class."

I was good in sports, which kept most of the bullies away, but I stuttered, which affected my spelling and reading. The kids called me "ears" because mine stuck out very prominently on my head. The doctor said it was because the cartilage behind my ears wasn't aligned right. They used to say I looked like a taxi cab coming down the street with its doors open.

My math was good until I took algebra, and with my poor reading comprehension I just could not solve the word problems. Not being able to extract the correct formula to solve the problem, and having no one to help me because Mom never learned algebra, I couldn't do my homework, which led to poor grades.

Growing up in Hagerstown, Maryland during the 40s and 50s was a lonely time for me. However, children grow up and each has a different road to travel before God takes His harvest. I hope this crop is what He is looking for.

Christmas In The Eyes Of A Child.

When I was a child living on the Public Square in Hagerstown, Maryland, it was like the whole town revolved around my family, especially at Christmas time. Christmas has always been a special time during my life, and I remember how the city would place a huge Christmas tree in the middle of the Public Square. Mother's beauty salon overlooked the Public Square, and my mother, Pauline, and my sister, Paulette and I lived in an apartment connected to the beauty salon. At night when the salon was closed, which was late due to the season, I sat in the window looking out over the Public Square.

The lights from below, especially from the Christmas tree, would explode in colors on the walls behind me in the salon. People were busy going in and out of the stores below, carrying their newly purchased treasures for unsuspecting family and friends. You could feel the hustle, bustle and joy that seemed to come with the new falling snow and excitement of the season. A child's excitement would swell inside me as I saw the many brightly wrapped presents going up and down the streets, and in and out of cars and buses.

We had our own Christmas tree with an city scene beneath it. There was a train that smoked and whistled as the main light on the front of the engine lit the tunnel as it went through and went behind the tree. There was also a miniature town with cars, houses, people, animals, and even live gold fish in a wash tub posing as a lake for the scene. There was cotton with glitter for snow, and a church that had lights inside making the glittery cotton sparkle like newly fallen snow.

Some presents were always under or by the tree around Christmas time. Haddy, our housekeeper, would take my sister and me out to buy presents for Mom and other family members, and we would place these by the tree. There was something exciting about discovering a present by the tree that you never saw before; the wonder of it all just filled my mind with curiosity.

Anyway, I looked out the window with amazement at the beautiful Christmas tree, which had a large star at the top that was at eye level to me. I envisioned myself flying around the top of this tree like an angel looking down at the people, even though at times mom had said, "He is no angel." The atmosphere made me daydream that I was off to Santa's workshop opening and making mountains of presents. I knew that Santa didn't really come from the North Pole but it was fun visiting him anyway.

Yes, I can remember the Christmas tree in the middle of Hagerstown's Public Square. I just hope the spirit that was given to me back in 1949 will always embrace our children in the future. "Merry Christmas to all and to all a good night," as Tiny Tim would say.

Black Is Beautiful

When I was a child, about six years old, I lived in an apartment with my mother and sister. We lived in the center of Hagerstown, Maryland in a place called The Public Square. This was where Potomac Avenue and Washington Street crossed each other, both leading out of town going north, south, east, and west.

Mom worked at and managed a beauty parlor that was connected to the apartment where we lived. Both were located on the top floor of the Mathis building which overlooked the square. It was a perfect place to watch the annual Halloween, Christmas, and New Year's parades. The judging booth and viewing stands were right beneath us in the square. and we had all the conveniences of home, literally, during the parades.

Since Mom had to work to support Paulete and myself, she hired a housemaid and cook to take care of the house while she was working in Paulette's Beauty Parlor; she had named the beauty parlor after my sister. The housekeeper and cook was a Negro, which was a term used to describe a black person, or African American, in the 1950s. I don't know her real name, but we called her Haddy, and I will always remember her kindness and love for Paulette and me.

When Mom used to take a break, she would sit down with Haddy and talk to her. Mom tried to get her to sit down and eat with us one time, but Haddy said, "that wasn't her place, to sit with white forks." Haddy told Mom about her son who treated her pretty bad, stealing from her and worse. She was a beautiful person and loved us kids as if we were her own. She never had too much money, and Mom could not pay her much, but with what little money she had she would take us kids on the city bus. Sometimes she would buy us some candy, and we would ride the bus completely around its circuit, getting off where we had gotten on. There were four different bus routes going around the city from The Public Square, and we would take a different one each time, seeing the whole city of Hagerstown. We went from Hager Park, to Pang Born Park, all for 25 cents; kids rode for free.

When Mom got married, we moved away to Interval Road in Hagerstown. Mom opened up another beauty parlor on the other side of town, and we never saw or heard from Haddy again. She was one lady that proved to me that black is beautiful, and I will never forget the bus rides we had together when I was a child.

The Right Church

My first memory of a church was when I stayed with the Barnhart family near Greencastle, Pennsylvania. I must have been four or five years old. Mrs. Barnhart, who I called Mom, though she was no relation to me, would take me to a little country church at night. I would lie on the pews and play with the hard gum stuck under the seats left by previous worshipers. I would listen to the music and try to sing along from time to time.

I remember going with the Barnhart family to a tent meeting and going up front and singing with Barbara and Patsy Barnhart, Mrs. Barnhart's daughters. We sang a song we had practiced at home, "Jesus Is a Wonderful Savior." Even today, I can remember the words to that song and almost see the tent and smell the dust in the air of that meeting in progress. I remember the old black cars, some with rumble seats and wide whitewall tires with spokes in the hubs and round hubcaps. There was preaching of the healing power of Jesus, how much God loved us, the miracles He had preformed, and salvation by grace. It was all being shouted by the evangelist that had come to town, and this truth was confirmed by the people at the meeting with a "Hallelujah Amen." People I had never seen before came up front and hugged and kissed me after the song, and I remember enjoying the affection, some given for my singing, but mostly for my youth I think.

After that, my next remembrance is of going to a Catholic School in Hagerstown with mom working in a beauty parlor just across the street. This Catholic church had a school and a playground behind it. I was about six or seven years old then. The Church had stained glass windows and a life sized model of Jesus on a cross, with thorns on His head, and painted blood running down His face. And to His right side at the foot of the cross was a table with lots of candles in red glasses, some lit and others not. A few larger candles on stands were placed by statues up front and near the wall in yellow and red glass containers. I remember incense burning somewhere making a pleasant smell in the church, and the lights were dim making the candles give a warm comfortable feeling in the sanctuary. My class and I were taken to the sanctuary where we would say our "hail Marys," followed by the Lord's Prayer. The school taught us to say this for each bead that was on our rosary that they had given us.

I then remember going to the Church of the Brethren in Hagerstown. I must have been eleven or twelve by then. I ended up getting baptized in this church. It was a larger church with a lot more people than the little country church back in Greencastle. I remember being dropped off for Sunday school class just before church. I didn't like that too much, because the Sunday school teacher made us read out loud, taking turns as we sat at the round table in class. I could not read very well, so I felt ashamed having to be helped with every other word from the Bible in front of all the other kids I hardly knew. Sometimes Mom dropped me off at the front

26

door of the church and I would go out the back door to the soda fountain drugstore at the top of the hill. That is where I waited for Sunday school to be over. Then I'd meet her back at the church when she would return from home, and we would go to the main church auditorium for the grownup service. This was just before and after Mom remarried that I attended that church.

All I remember about churches after that is getting married to Gayle Trollinger in a little Baptist church in Chapel Hill, North Carolina. I was twenty-four at the time. Gayle's family was Baptist, and since she was raised in that denomination we were married by a Baptist preacher, which was alright by me, having no denominational preference.

After that, we moved to South Carolina where I was stationed at Shaw Air Force Base. Not too much later, I received orders to go to Anderson Air Force Base in Guam. Gayle stayed with my mother and step-dad in Westminster, California until I could get a house for us near the base in Guam. Being an Airman First Class, I was authorized to bring my new bride with me, but only if I had a place for us to stay since base housing was not available for my pay grade. So I had to go find a house to live in, either until base housing became available, or I made the next pay grade of Staff Sergeant. Housing on Guam was horrible; off base housing was almost nonexistent.

To make things worse, buying a secondhand car on Guam, which I needed in order to get around, was almost impossible. Everyone drove what they called a "Guam Bomb," until their own cars arrived from the states by ship. Used cars were very hard to find. Finally, for five hundred dollars, I bought an old four door Plymouth that looked like an advertisement from a junk yard. You could see through the floorboards, and smoke would come in from the engine. The seat covers had expired long before, so I laid a blanket over them to cover the holes. It was not painted, but primed a rusty orange to keep it from rusting more and to match the rest of the rust already on the car. It used more oil than gas and I had to tie the back door shut with a rope. The car ran, but the brakes weren't the best, and parts for this car were both expensive and hard to find. But I was lucky to get it, and I needed a car to be able to look for a house and to get around the island. We had shipped our new Volkswagen out of San Pedro, California before I left for Guam, but it wasn't going to arrive for a couple of months, and I hoped to have a house by then to live in.

Being newly married, I wanted everything to be just right for my new bride, but the only house I could find was an unpainted tin duplex on cement stilts. I later found out that the stilts were because of termites that could eat a house up in a year. The Guamanian landlord, who lived at the other end of this two apartment duplex with his family, wanted five hundred fifty dollars a month for

28

rent, plus utilities. That was a lot of money for rent, especially for an Airman First Class who was not that high on the Air Force's pay scale.

The windows in the house had no glass, only screens with holes. The inside walls had not been painted and were bare used plywood. The kitchen cabinets were moldy with old peeling paint, and the bare plywood floors moved back and forth as you walked on them. It had one bedroom, a living room, a small kitchen, and a bathroom which was not attached to the duplex, and you could see the ground through a six inch open seam between the apartment and the bathroom. The shower was made of unpainted moldy cement, and the rest of the bathroom was made of rusty tin with a fiberglass roof. It was everything a new young bride (in a horror movie) would expect.

With the help of some friends from work, I put three coats of paint on everything, bought rugs for the floors and air-conditioners for two of the three windows. I filled the seam between the apartment and bathroom with paper and tape, and painted over it. The furniture also received a coat of paint and I sealed all holes including windows. Finally I bought a new mattress for the bed. The inside looked livable even if the outside was still rusty tin on cement stilts. The landlord did give me a month's free rent for fixing up his property. Besides, the outside matched my "Guam Bomb". I wondered though, what Gayle would think about being thirteen thousand miles from her mother on an island surrounded by sharks, beaches covered with flies, and with no windows to look out of. The beaches were beautiful if you could put up with the flies. There was a saying on Guam: "Guam is good by order of the base commander."

I remember getting on my knees in this newly painted apartment before Gayle arrived and praying, "Dear Lord if you really exist, I need you now." I wanted everything to be right for my new bride. At that time, with my eyes closed, I could see the picture of Christ standing at a door and the door opening and Him going in. This is when I first knew in my heart there was truly a God and His name was Jesus. Things were going to be ok!

I worked at the passenger terminal on base, and was in charge of handling all passenger flights in and out of the base. When Gayle's commercial flight arrived, I had her paged and offloaded ahead of all the other passengers onboard. She had made a friend named Frieda Perry, another newlywed whose husband, an Airman Second Class named Larry, worked in the aerial photography section on base. Larry had paid for his wife to come over to Guam out of his own pocket because the Air Force didn't authorize travel for an Airman Second Class's wife.

Larry went to a church located in the middle of the island called Calvary Baptist Church, which is where I started to become active again in church. I didn't know much about Bibles, but I knew I needed to learn more about this man called Jesus. Gayle was brought up in a religious home and knew about the different kinds of bibles, so I asked her to get me one that I could understand. My reading comprehension is very poor and the King James Version didn't make sense to me. She got me a Revised Standard Version, and I started reading in the beginning at Genesis. I seemed to know what it was going to say before I read it. I just surmised that God knew my reading ability and was giving me a little help. I later found out it was the Holy Spirit inside of me, and that the Word would never leave my heart.

A lot has happened since then, but I still believe there is a God and His son's name is Jesus. He saved me on Guam that day as I waited for my bride to come. Now I am a part of the bride, waiting for Him to appear. It's not the church you go to that matters, but who you believe in, and there is no other name under heaven by which you can be saved from your sins other than Jesus.

This is Larry and Frieda Perry who let me smoke in their house until the Lord told me to stop. Frieda would make ashtrays for me out of tin foil. I believe God sends people as you need them. Some people call these messengers from God "friends", "sweethearts", and/or "angels".

A Thanksgiving To Remember

It was Thanksgiving Day and Mom took Paulette, my sister, and I to Aunt Jessie's for Thanksgiving dinner. Aunt Jessie lived outside of Williamsport, Maryland with her husband Clifford Guessford and her four sons, Bob, Kaydon, Richard, and Nobel. My sister used to stay with the Guessfords and I would stay with the Barnharts while Mom worked in Hagerstown to support us. The Barnharts were no relation, but were a good Christian family who lived on a farm near Greencastle, Pennsylvania. Later, Mom decided to bring us back together to live with her in an apartment in Hagerstown in a place called the Public Square.

I always liked visiting relatives because there was always a warm loving feeling around family members. I enjoyed listening to stories the older boys told which excited my imagination, and I envied their wisdom and freedom. Also, I had two pets, a duck named Crackers and a chick I called Pee-Pee, that they kept for me since I lived in an apartment where pets weren't allowed. Although, we did keep them there in the apartment until they got too big.

At the previous Easter time, the five and dime

department store just down the street from where we lived sold baby bunnies, chicks and ducks. They dyed the chicks different colors, red, pink, green, blue, and they had the baby ducks swimming around in a wash tub in the store's showroom window. Mom didn't want to bring them back to the apartment, but a little boy can be very persuasive when he's all cooped up in an apartment with no dad to explain things to him. Besides, they looked so cute. I told her the duck could use the bathtub and that I would take care of them, cleaning up any messes they would make. Please! Please!

We got one duck and two pee-pees, which is what I called the baby chicks because of the sound they made. We got a pink chick and a blue chick; the duck didn't have any dye on him and was all yellow, and his tail would twitch back and forth, which I thought was funny. After awhile they got bigger and, sadly, the blue pee-pee died. We buried him in a shoe box out behind the apartment near the alley. But the pink pee-pee would follow the duck around; anywhere the duck would go the pink pee-pee would follow.

Mom said they were getting too big to stay in the apartment, so we took them to Aunt Jessie and Uncle Clifford who lived in the country. Uncle Clifford put the pee-pee in with the other chickens he had, and he found an old wash tub for the duck to swim in. They played, ate, and slept together, staying away from the other chickens. As a matter of fact, the duck would protect his friend from the other chickens in the hen house, including the rooster. Uncle Clifford, who we called Pop, didn't like the duck because the hens wouldn't lay as much since the duck came. And the duck would fight with the rooster if he came near my pee-pee which was a large white chicken by then. The duck was also white and had gotten a lot bigger than the rooster. Anyway, the duck was more in charge of the hen house than the rooster and Pop didn't seem to like that.

When we arrived at Aunt Jessie and Uncle Clifford's for Thanksgiving, the boys were out hunting rabbits in a field behind the house, and the house smelled of food being cooked. There was homemade fudge on the coffee table and I took a piece. Mom said I could have only one because we were going to eat soon. Then she and my sister went off to the kitchen to help with dinner.

I took another piece of fudge and ran outside to see if my cousins were back yet, and to look in on my pets. Richard was coming up the hill looking kind of tired with his shotgun broke open and hanging over his arm. Only Richard and Kaydon went hunting and I didn't know where Nobel and Bob were. Richard said they had gotten their limit and he began to skin the rabbits. He placed their hind legs up on two nails at the top of a wooded plank and pulled the skin off after first cutting around the legs to free the skin. I watched, wanting to know everything to do when I was old enough to go hunting.

We talked and went into the house to get ready for dinner. There was a long table that almost covered the entire room, and it was covered with food. The Guessfords were not a rich family but there was always plenty to eat, and everyone I ever knew in my family was a good cook. I sat on a couple of pillows on an old wooden chair so my head and shoulders were up above my plate. Then Mom took my plate and put mashed potatoes and gravy on it, which I loved, and then sweet potatoes and some cranberry relish, which was also a favorite of mine. I notice that some people refer to sweet potatoes as candied yams, and what I liked best about them were the nuts and pineapples in them. Mom then passed the plate down to Pop who was serving the meat and I said, "Give me some turkey, white meat please." Then it seemed to get silent around the table when Pop said, "We aren't having turkey this year, only duck." I had never had duck before. Then Pop explained that he couldn't keep the duck anymore because of the fighting with the rooster in the hen house, and because the hens were not laying well. That's why he had decided to get rid of the duck and the chicken that year.

I didn't cry, but to this day I don't like chicken all that well, and the only duck I have ever eaten was in China. The facts may be a little off, but I remember what they did to my pets.

Peaty

Living in the projects on the northeastern side of Hagerstown, and learning to fend for myself wasn't easy, but that's what I did when I was about seven years old.

My dad had left my mother when I was about three, leaving Mom to raise two children on her own. There were three of us, but my baby brother, Donnie Lee, died of pneumonia when he was just a year old.

All this made for a very insecure childhood, but I had a parakeet for a pet whose name was Peaty. Having a pet seemed to help with my insecurities, maybe because I felt in charge of something for a change. Mom and I named him Peaty because we wanted a talking parakeet, and we learned that a male bird with four black dots around its neck could pronounce words starting with "P" easier. The four black dots supposedly indicated that the bird was older and would talk more, trying to gain the favor of any female bird. And we also were told that a female bird doesn't talk as much as a male one.

Peaty was green and yellow, and I would always say things to him like, "Pretty Peaty, pretty bird". It wasn't long before he would repeat what I said. Sometimes he'd say "Pretty, pretty Peaty, pretty, pretty bird." Male ego I guess.

Peaty loved water and he loved looking at himself in the mirror. We believed that when he saw himself, he thought it was another bird and he tried to mate with it. So, in his cage we put a glass of water with a mirror beside it, and he used to talk to the mirror all

36

day long saying, "Pretty Peaty, pretty bird." And he would splash in the glass of water as if he was taking a bath. After he lived with us for awhile I would let him out of his cage and he would fly around the house. His favorite spot though, was on that glass of water which we kept in the kitchen by his cage. It was warmer there with more light from the kitchen windows.

While we watched television in the living room, Peaty would sometimes fly in and sit on the drapes over the front windows. Then, after awhile he would fly down to me where I lay on the couch and sit on my ear, going around it like he did on the glass of water saying, "Pretty Peaty, pretty bird."

He had one habit that Mom didn't like. For some reason he would put seeds in my ears while going around, biting on my ear and talking. Sometimes his biting hurt, but I thought it was neat to have him do his little dance on my ear, so I didn't object much. Mom complained while she cleaned the seeds out of my ears, but she loved the bird as much as I did.

When Mom fixed dinner for my sister, Paulette, and I, Peaty would fly down on the table while we were eating sometimes and walk through the butter, which made Mom mad. She was thinking about clipping his wings. In the mornings Peaty would fly upstairs and into my room, then land on my ear and do his little dance, waking me up for school; Mom liked that. When Mom came home from work, Peaty would fly and land on her shoulder as she came in the front door, as if welcoming her home.

He would always sit on your finger if you placed it under his breast, but he was messy. Feathers were everywhere and sometimes

Peaty would poop down the back of the drapes. I helped to keep the house clean though, and he became part of the family.

One day Mom came home from work and Peaty flew onto her shoulder, but she forgot he was there and when she walked back outside later to go to the car, Peaty flew away over the housing complex and out of sight. We all cried after driving around for hours trying to find him again with no success.

The next day in school however, I heard a boy talking about this dirty green bird that flew into his mother's upstairs bedroom window, landed on her vanity cabinet and started talking to itself in front of her mirror. Hearing that, I got so excited. But I didn't want to upset the boy so I waited until after school, and then ran all the way home and told Mom all about what this boy had said. Mom got hold of the teacher and found out where the boy lived then we drove over to his house, which was four miles away, and sure enough it was Peaty. The boy didn't want to give him up, but his Mom saw how much we missed the bird and she let us have him.

Mom clipped his wings after that, but they grew back and eventually the same thing happened again. Unfortunately it was a lot colder outside the second time, and we never did find Peaty after that. As a child, I loved that bird, and even today I think about and miss him.

Many years later, when she lived in Idaho, Mom had another parakeet. It was blue and white and she also taught it to talk. It too became part of the family. It finally died of old age which was difficult. Losing a family member is hard, no matter how it happens.

This is my Mother at 18 years old, and this is my daughter, April, at 18 years.

This is Perky, Mom's parakeet. He was out of his cage one day and flew down to the kitchen stove and ate some grease around the burners which had cleanser in it and die of food poisoning. We cried!

The Sting Of A Spelling Bee.

Attending School in early years was not what moms and dads would have liked to believe. You've probably heard of "only the strong survive." Well it seemed to me that only the gifted and politically affluent received what everyone was paying for. An education should have equally applied to all, but school gave me a complex. I felt alienated from other kids because I was dumber. Or was I? I was always the first to sit down during our daily spelling bees, which made me feel like I was dumber than everyone else. It gave me a complex and made me become a shy little introvert. I later found out that I could not pronounce words correctly because I stuttered, and being unable to pronounce words correctly was the main reason I could not spell them. My teacher was no help. While lauding over her favorite students, she told me to look up the words in the dictionary. It didn't occur to her that if you can't sound out a word, a dictionary is of little use. At the end of the year I was still sitting while others were standing and spelling "cannonball." They were so smart. I guess I got stung by the bee.

40

At Mother's Request

Writing Your Memoirs
November 4, 2005

Jim Patrick Renee Bill John Gary
Marie Anita Barbara Evelyn

"Gary you should write a book about the things you have done," my mother kept saying, each time I went to visit her in Sandpoint, Idaho. And like always, I would tell her, "I can't even spell my name sometimes, much less write a book." She would then tell me that there are people that will write it for you, all you have to do is tell them "the facts, man, nothing but the facts." She said it just like Joe Friday from the television program, Dragnet, and then she smiled. So, in the back of my mind I started thinking about how I could write the book that she suggested.

Not long after returning home, I received an advertisement from the College Of Southern Maryland, Adult Plus division, listing a _Writing Your Memoirs_ class. It seemed to me that breaking a task, like writing a book, into smaller parts would be easier than tackling the whole thing all at once, so I signed up.

The class was instructed by a Mrs. Renee Nelson, who I found out later not only taught memoir construction, but had a master's degree in writing, and one hell of an interest in teaching. So, I attended my first class at Richard Clark Senior Center in La Plata, Maryland where I was greeted and welcomed by a mechanical life-like picture of Elvis Presley inside the front door.

In all there were nine students registered for the course. The first one I met was name Bill, who I liked right away. He was an ex-military man and easy to talk to. He bought me a canned coke, which I put a pack of Planter's peanuts in. He looked at me kind of funny but didn't say anything. I had seen another college student do it once, so I tried it and discovered I liked the taste of the salted peanuts marinated in coke. Then there was Jim, an intelligent

 and kind man, and Patrick, a very sensitive individual. There was also John, who seemed nice, but who I didn't get to know well. The ladies' names were Marie, a good looking goal setter who always had a suggestion; Evelyn, a kind and thoughtful woman, a lot like my mother; Barbara, a good person to have in your corner in case of an intellectual fight; and Anita, a Southern aristocratic lady who said she had never had a birthday cake. Well I did not think that was any

way to treat a Southern lady, and besides, her birthday was coming up. So I bought her a birthday cake with candles, and our teacher and classmates chipped in with party favors, napkins, and other items for the party to celebrate her 75th birthday.

During one of the classes I asked Mrs. Nelson how many memoirs I would need to make a book and she said that it would be nice to have at least seventy or so. I told her what I had in mind, but that I couldn't spell and my grammar was out the door. She said that shouldn't stop me from writing, and she offered to edit the book for me. So, at mother's request I wrote a book and also had a party. Thanks to Mom and Mrs. Nelson, a Southern lady was shown some hospitality, and I became an author.

Vacation

My step-dad, mother, sister, and I were on our yearly vacation and I was eight years old. Bill, my step-dad, was the only father I ever knew. My biological father had run away from us when I was three years old and I never knew him. So I called Bill "Dad."

We were on the Pennsylvania Turnpike traveling northwest towards Minnesota, and I was in my favorite place, the back seat window of our new Mercury, looking up at the stars. Being in the window wasn't a safe place to be, but Mom and Dad didn't seem to mind, they were busy talking about Dad's family in Minnesota. My sister was asleep on the back seat, and with me laying in the back window we could both stretch our legs.

I saw the big dipper and then the little dipper. I began searching for Leo the Lion since August is my birthday month, but Leo is a little harder to find. Lying up against the back window I saw a deep dark blue sky and millions of stars shinning just for me. I felt safe and secure with my family for some reason. I remember thinking that God was looking back at me saying, "Have a wonderful vacation." I just knew this was going to be the best vacation yet. After all, not many people hear from God, unless they seek Him with all their hearts, or as the Bible says, "Seek and ye shall find."

My Love For The Ocean.

The sea has always been a special place for me. I remember as a child going to Ocean City, Maryland with my mother. I built a sand castle on the beach, and we watched as the waves and the incoming tide leveled my all day creation. This happened during the heat of the day, making room for the next kid to come with his or her shovel and pail.

I remember burying my mom in the sand, leaving only her head out so she could breathe, or she would bury me, and I recall how cool the sand felt then as I lay beneath it. Afterwards, although I took a shower, I was not able to get all the sand out from under my bathing suit, and out of my ears, nose, and other openings in my body.

Sometimes the sand was so hot I could barely walk on it. As I walked back across the beach from the ocean, it got hotter and hotter until I finally had to run and jump up onto the steps leading to the boardwalk, which was also hot with its tarred planks and iron nails. I looked for shaded areas on the boardwalk, near the stores, to give my feet some rest and relief from the intensive heat generated by the sun. Flip-flops helped, especially on the boardwalk, but on the beach the hot sand swallowed my feet and came up over the sponge bottoms of the flip-flops and onto my tender skin, making me run to higher ground looking for shade. Sometimes my flip-flops came off my feet and I had to stop and be tortured until I retrieved my footwear from the hot sand. Once on the boardwalk my flip flops moved up and down, scratching me as I walked because of the abrasive sand between my toes that I had failed to brush off.

This was just one lesson I was taught as a child as I learned to cope with the beach environment. I had many other experiences as well that left me with memories of the sea, the sound of the crashing waves on the beach, the feel of the scorching summer sun on the sand, the sound of ever screeching seagulls crying for food, and the taste and sight of multicolored salt water taffy provided by the boardwalk store vendors.

I remember while standing in the water the waves would pull sand, sea shells and other things across my feet towards the shore and then back over them again and out to sea. I sometimes wondered what the other things were and how many sharks were in the water. I used to dive into the waves, smashing my head against the incoming wall of water and coming out the other side. The wave passed by me and hurried to the shore, then left a carpet of white sea foam as it returned to the ocean.

As I grew older it was a different type of beach I remember. This beach was one of girls in bathing suits, body surfing, sun tans, and volleyball. Redondo Beach in California was the perfect place to meet these girls and to body surf or just get a sun tan. And in the evenings, as I got older still, I found that Palos Verdes, California was the perfect place to take these girls. Los Angeles, and most of the cities of southern California, could be seen from Palos Verdes which was located high on a hill. This was also where the teenagers parked at night, and it was nicknamed "Lovers Lane" by most of the younger generation.

After picking up some beer or wine, if I could get it (being only 16 years old), we'd drive to Lover's Lane and watch the lights of the cities as they glowed beneath us. That is where this adolescent furthered his relationship with the opposite sex, but never lost his chastity. After a little progress or trust was established between my date and I, we sometimes walked along the ocean near Redondo Beach. This was very romantic, but very cold at night with the breeze off the Pacific Ocean and the dampness in the air. It gave me a chance to be the type of gentleman promoted in the movies and I'd offer my jacket to my date if she hadn't brought her own sweater. To help dispel the dampness, I exercised more courage by putting my arm around her as we walked along the secluded beach.

There were some years when the ocean waves had a fluorescent glow which was caused by a sea plant in the water. Some people called it "red tide"; I just called it beautiful. It was like something from a Walt Disney movie where the mermaid turns into sea foam, sparkling in the moonlight on top of the waves that spread her out over the incoming water for young lovers to spoon by. During the day however, the red tide made the waves look rusty, muddy and uninviting. It also smelled bad for the most part, but at night the air was made fresher by the coolness, and the soft glow from the waves and sea form created a very romantic atmosphere.

Another remarkable time along the beach was when the grunions were running. These little fish would spawn along the beach during high tide, laying their eggs in the sand and returning to the water they came from during a full moon. Imagine thousands of fish caring not for their safety, only knowing what they must do as their parents did before them. Many of them were being preyed upon by birds and other predators looking for a late evening snack. But nature must have its way, and the time had come for the grunions to propagate in the sand.

Later, when I turned 17 years old in Downey, California, which is near Long Beach, I joined the Air Force, leaving California for San Antonio, Texas and basic training. For part of my twenty-two years in the service I was stationed at Anderson Air Force Base on the island of Guam, in the Pacific, where I learned how to scuba dive and snorkel for sea shells. If you ever want to see a new color, go snorkeling in the Pacific Ocean. Between the fish and the coral there are colors I don't think there are names for. Most of the visible sea life is within a thirty foot depth of water, and in these thirty feet are the most beautiful creatures and habitat I have ever seen. The fish are not afraid of people, and their environment is breathtaking. I was stationed on Guam for a year and my love for the ocean there, and the coral reefs around it, is beyond words. Even the sky on this island seemed to come down and excite my mind with its color and closeness. Diving on Guam's reefs gave me a relaxing frame of mind, allowing me to shut out the outside world and float or swim in a real fantasy environment filled with sea creatures of many colors and shapes.

While I snorkeled, making the effort to come up for air was a nuisance as I enjoyed being beneath the surface and exploring new unknowns. The experience made me want to use scuba diving equipment to enable me to stay longer to search for the hidden treasures that may lie beneath the waves. When I scanned the world below as I floated and snorkeled on top of the water, going up and down with each new wave, I felt my mind wishing to join the world below and be part of the mysteries it held.

Best Friends Who & How

Billy Baker was my best friend when I was a teenager and I will never forget the way we met. He was the biggest bully in the neighborhood.

I had just moved to a new part of town, and my mother had just started dating Allen Harball, who happened to be Billy's uncle. Mom and I had just returned from church, and I was all dressed up in a new suit Mom had bought for me. We went over to Mr. Harball's house because he was going to take us on a picnic. When we got there, Mr. Harball wasn't ready yet, so I told Mom I was going out back to look around. It had rained the night before, so Mom told me not to get dirty because we would be leaving soon.

Out in the back yard was Billy Baker and two other kids, who he called the twins. Billy had his play clothes on—blue jeans, checkered shirt, and sneakers—and when he saw me all dressed up, he must have thought I was some kind of momma's boy. He came over and grabbed hold of me to show off in front of his friends. I wasn't much of a fighter, but I did fairly well in wrestling, so when he grabbed me, I flipped him over into a mud puddle. He just sat there, looked up at me, and laughed. We have been the best of friends ever since. In fact, he is now a detective with the Hagerstown Police Department and has been for 40 years. He has helped many young men overcome their fears from bullies like him.

Billy

61

        We came in second place that year after playing one of the best basketball games Hagerstown had ever seen. Our whole main string, except for Billy, fowled out and we only lost by 2 points. It was a long walk home that night. Billy attempted a shot from half court that bounce off the rim of the basket as the whistle blew. No one was there to see me play that night, I being the last to fowl out and one of the high scorers of the evening. That put the Lions Club in first place and the Alsatia Club in second place for the league that year. No Dad, so sad.

God Sent A Man.

As a kid growing up in Hagerstown, Maryland I had to fend for myself since I had no father for guidance and a mother who had to work as a beautician to support herself, my sister Paulette, and I. Mom farmed us out once when we were younger, sending my sister to live with Jessie Guessford, our aunt in Williamsport, Maryland, and me to Mom Barnhart's (that is what I called her, but she was no relation to our family). They were a good Christian family living on a small farm in the country between Hagerstown, Maryland and Greencastle, Pennsylvania. I remember missing my mother and hitchhiking back to Mom's apartment from the Barnhart's. I must have been 6 or 7 years old, maybe younger. A farmer going into Hagerstown to market picked me up and let me off near the apartment. I remembered how to get to the apartment once I got to Hagerstown. I waited outside where there was a playground in back of the apartment complex, until Mom got home from work. She decided to let me stay with her from then on. It was school in the morning and when Mom came home from work she made dinner and we watched television. Later she brought my sister back from Aunt Jessie's.

As a kid I learned early that you made friends real easy if you had something they wanted, like ice cream, candy, bicycles, or money, but I didn't have any way then to get those things, with the exception of stealing. So I stole money from my mother's purse and took the money down to the corner store to buy ice cream for all the kids. Mom didn't keep track of the money from her beauty parlor profits closely, but I do think she wondered what happened to some of the money sometimes. Raising children when you are young and by yourself is not an easy task. The ice cream and candy made me popular among the kids and I didn't have to worry about getting beat up by the bigger kids, which gave me a sense of security. I was learning how to take care of myself in this world I lived in. The projects, which is what we called the apartment complex, was a breeding ground for, "The Good, The Bad, and The Ugly." Low cost housing was all my mother could afford, but we were together and I needed that. Paulette, my sister is four years younger than me and I felt a responsibility for her even at that young age. One time some boys found a dead snake in the play ground and threw it on my sister while she was swinging in the playground out behind our apartment. She came home crying and told me what had happened. I found the snake and put it in their mailbox, which was a slit in their apartment entrance door. It was a get even world for kids who had no rooted family to look after them.

Parents that don't have time to look after their kids, let their kids look after themselves. And I did what I thought was right for a nine year old. Mom saw this and I believe that is the reason she got married again. Her customers lined her up with a man name William Reineke who was raised in Minneapolis, Minnesota but born in Elton, South Dakota. He had been in the army and received the Purple Heart for a bomb that exploded next to a vehicle he was riding in, killing the driver and wounding him. He was a member of the Elk's lodge and used to take us to their picnics. When Mom met him, he worked as a quality control representative for Fairchild Aircraft. They seemed to need each other and he was the best thing to come into our lives. It was as if God sent a man to fill the gap. But at that time he was just another person between my mother and me, adding to my insecurity.

Breaking In A Step-Dad.

I was fifteen years old and Mom and my new step-dad, Bill, wanted to ship me off to Carlisle Military School, in Bamberg, South Carolina. Mom was working, pregnant, and had little time for watching a fifteen-year-old independent teenager. Bill was trying his best to get along with me, but between his job, which required him to be gone a lot, and my "want to do it my way" attitude, we just weren't walking the same path, so to speak, as many teenagers with step-dads know. They thought putting me in military school would teach me some discipline and respect for authority.

The idea came up after I had stolen our Studebaker car out of the garage while Bill was on a trip. We had two cars, a two-door, yellow and black 1955 Cadillac, and a four-door, dark green 1950 Studebaker. I had taken the Studebaker out one night and gone on a joyride with some of my friends. The problem being, on returning home, the car had to be backed into the garage as it was parked before. The driveway leading into the garage was loose stone, slanting uphill, and the Studebaker was a three-speed stick-shift being driven by an inexperienced driver with no license. My friends and I had pushed it out of the garage with no lights on to keep from being seen. Bill always backed "his" cars into the garage. His main car was the Cadillac and Mom drove the Studebaker. I took the Studebaker because Bill is a perfectionist and he would know if you even opened the door of the Cadillac. Therefore, Mom's car was the target.

Bill had just built this two-car garage behind our house on Interval Road in Hagerstown, Maryland, and he gave me fifty dollars to put two coats of white paint on the outside cement block walls and white trim around the windows and doors. I did a good job if I must say so myself; it took a lot of paint and two days to finish.

Anyway, with the lights out I tried to back the car into the garage because it was too heavy to push up hill in loose stone. When I put it in reverse and let the clutch out, the engine stalled. I did it again and the engine stalled again. I was getting nervous and mad at this crazy car for not doing what I wanted it to do. Besides, I was looking bad in front of my friends since I was supposed to be the hot shot driver. I gave it some gas and popped the clutch, and stones flew out from under the tires hitting everything. I lost control of the steering and hit the side of the garage door, bending the car door in and tearing the side of the garage door up. The white paint had looked better on the garage door than it now looked on the car door. I didn't know what else to do, but I knew I was in trouble. My friends went home, and I closed the garage door and went inside to bed. Talk about a sleepless night; I may have gotten an hour or so of sleep. The next day I went to school by bus like nothing had happened. Bill was still away on a business trip and Mom hadn't seen the car yet.

Well at school I was big and brave around my friends, talking about the night before and how that old six cylinder Studebaker could only do ninety-two miles per hour. I bragged about speeding on an old country road, coming upon a main highway at the top of a hill with a stop sign, slamming on the breaks and sliding across a four-lane highway sideways. I laughed about finally coming to a complete stop on the other side, the car heading in the same direction as we had come from. But in the back of my mind, I was waiting for that call from the principal's office to say that someone wanted to talk to me. I didn't even think about how lucky my friends and I were to even be alive.

That day went by fast, and I went home almost forgetting about what I had done, me being the big wheel of the day with my friends. I went into the house and Mom was in the kitchen fixing dinner. She didn't even look up but said, "Gary, Bill wants to see you in the garage." That seemed like the longest walk to the garage I had ever taken. The garage had a side entrance door leading to the house which I walked through, closing it behind me. Bill looked at me, walked over to the main garage door by the Studebaker and slowly pulled it shut. He turned and slowly walked toward me. He stopped in front of me, looking down and said, "When in the **G__D__ Hell** are you going to stop your **G__D__ F_____** around?" Needless to say, the words got louder and the language worse. I felt like I was vibrating into the ground with this huge, out of control man looking down and shouting at me. Most of the words I knew, but there were a few that were new to me. Well, after that I was in my room, grounded for an unlimited time, and awaiting punishment from behind, if you know what I mean.

It sure was hard to break in a step-dad. Maybe military school wasn't a bad idea, I thought. At last it would get me out of the house again.

Mom and Dad

For Friendship's Sake

I was 15 years old and had just moved from Bamberg, South Carolina to 149th Street in Gardena, California. I was trying to make friends in this new area when Bob Marshall, a boy I had met at Perry Junior High School in Gardena, had come over to my house. My mother Pauline, step-dad, Bill, sister, Paulette and baby brother, Willis were out shopping in Long Beach, and wouldn't be back until later that day.

Back then, being "bad" or "cool" for a teenager was the in thing and Bob seemed to be pretty bad and cool to me; I wanted him to like me. Besides, to be cool, you had to either be a surfer or a hoe-dad. A hoe-dad was like Elvis, with styled hair, blue suede shoes, jeans you could stand up in the corner, and a cigarette hanging out the side of your mouth while you snapped a Zippo lighter with two fingers to open it. Kind of like the Fonz character from "Happy Days." Surfers, on the other hand, would hang ten on their surfboards, or body surf if they didn't have surfboards, which were few and far between back then. Rubber rafts and body surfing were the main rides then; surfboards came later, with the Beach Boys.

Trying to get on his good side, I asked Bob if he wanted something to drink, meaning coke, root beer, or 7-up. He walked over to the refrigerator and opened it up saying, "What do you have?" I didn't see anything wrong with that until he pulled out Mom and Dad's Mogen David wine and said, "Where are the glasses?" I said, "I don't think we should drink that. It is Mom's and Dad's," and he said, "We won't drink much; they will never know it's missing." Well a little wouldn't hurt, I thought, besides he was probably right, they would never miss it. I had drunk some of Dad's Balantine's Scotch before, replacing it with water, and gotten away with it, so I thought I'd show Bob that I was no sissy. I said, "I know where there is some whiskey too," thinking of doing the same thing with the whiskey as I did with the scotch. He looked at me and said, "Go get it." I did, and when I got back with the whiskey there were two water glasses, two thirds full of wine, sitting on the kitchen table. Bob took the whiskey and topped the glasses off, filling them to the rim. He took one glass and I took the other and we toasted to friendship. It wasn't so bad after the third or fourth gulp; by then my face was kind of numb. We drank our drinks, trying to keep up with one another, and I suddenly got tired. Bob said he was going into the living room to take a nap on the couch. I wasn't feeling too good, and a nap sounded like a good idea, so I just laid my head down on the kitchen table.

The next thing I remember was mom coming into the kitchen and saying, "Gary are you ok?" I raised my head up, just in time to see her go back outside and holler, "Bill, Gary is drunk!" She then came back into the house and found Bob on the couch and disgustingly said, "Bob, you get your hat and never knock on these premises again." Bob replied, slurring his words, "That's ok with me lady, there is just one problem." Mom, even angrier said, "And what's that?" Bob in a quiet response, still slurring each word said, "I don't have a hat." Things went downhill fast from then on. Bob was out the door and Bill had me in his arms carrying me to the bathroom. He put me in the bathtub and turned on the shower, cold water, at full force. I started slipping and sliding trying to get out of that bathtub. Dad probably thought I was going to break my neck, but he wouldn't let me out. He told me to dry off and go to my room and stay there. I dried off, went into my room and fell on the bed. One hour went by and mom opened the door to tell me supper was ready and to wash my hands and come to the table. Now food was the last thing on my mind at that time, but they made me come to the table and eat.

That was the last time I ever got drunk in front of my parents, and to this day I don't know what ever happened to Bob, or if he ever got a hat.

My First Real Job.

Brad

The first real job that I ever had was the only job I was ever fired from. I was a teenager in Gardena, California and school was out for the summer, but I didn't have any money to maintain my lifestyle of beach, basketball, or party time. My step-dad, Bill Reineke, used to give me an allowance, which I had to work for. It was something like 25 cents for making my bed, 10 cents for sweeping the kitchen floor, 25 cents for vacuuming the living room, 25 cents for carrying out the trash, and 25 cents for washing the dishes. Of course my sister got the same for drying the dishes, or for doing whatever I had not done around the house.

But Mom and Dad thought I was getting too big for that kind of work and that I should get a summer job, so they gave me pep talks about going out and finding one for that summer. A lot of my friends already had part-time work, but they were always too busy to go out and have fun. I didn't think that working part-time was for me, because it would cut into my social time, and it would prevent summer vacation from being just that, summer vacation.

But I needed the money so I figured that the newspaper was a good place to start my job search. I noticed that a garden nursery in Gardena, not too far from the house, was hiring, and they said the pay was good. Dad said that he would have "hauled shit in buckets" for that kind of money at my age, then he offered to drive me down to fill out an application. Instead, I decided to call Brad, a good friend of mine who was also looking for a job. He needed the money for insurance for his car, not to mention gas money, drive-in movie money, beach money, girlfriend money, and just plain spending money.

A car was in my dreams, but far from being in my pocketbook, and I was still a little young for a driver's license. So, I used to hitchhike to the beach with my friends, scope out the chicks, and do a little body surfing. Later, when I started to get hungry, my friends and I would stop by a drive-in hamburger stand where another friend of mine, named Jim, worked. He would give us the extra hamburgers and fries that people hadn't ordered that would be thrown away. If I had a date and wanted to go to the drive-in, I would line up my friend, one who had a car, with a date. Or sometimes I'd get into the trunk of the car and sneak into the drive-in, but I only did that with the guys. Sometimes we'd get some old wino to buy us some beer, giving him a few dollars to do it. For money we'd go around and collect pop bottles to take to the store for deposit. Usually it gave us enough money to buy some fries and a drink at the beach, and put gas into the car. Our allowance was another source of income. Sometimes we would cut grass, which would pay enough for a date. But a part-time job was something new for me. Mom said I could use the money I'd earn to buy some of my clothes for school.

Anyway, Brad picked me up and we saw the foreman at the nursery who asked us a few questions. He gave us forms that needed to be signed by our parents so we could work and get a Social

Security Number. I listed my name as Gary Reineke, which was my stepfather's last name, so even today my first W-2 form has Gary Reineke on it, though I have never been adopted. The Social Security Office has never corrected it either, even though I told them about it. Brad and I returned the signed forms and reported to work bright and early the following morning.

We were given the job of filling pallets for planting. These were wooden boxes, 4 inches high and 2 feet long, by 2 feet wide. After we filled these pallets with fertile dirt, they were placed in a greenhouse and seeded. The nursery was fairly large so there were a lot of greenhouses, and when the plants were larger they were taken outside to be replanted for shipment at a later date. We'd fill the pallets and place them on a large wooden pallet, and then a forklift would come by and carry them into a greenhouse for seeding. After we had filled the large pallet with small seeding pallets, we went over and dumped out the used dirt from the old seeding pallets and placed them upside down in a stack. That's where they stayed until they needed to be refilled again with new fertile soil for reseeding. So it was put in the dirt, dump out the dirt, and not too much mental ability was needed.

After about a month, Brad and I were used to the routine. There seemed to be more dumping than filling, so we stacked the empty seeding pallets in a square about 7 feet high and 6 feet wide, leaving room in the middle. That's where we took breaks to have a smoke or just hang out for awhile, because no one could see us in the middle of the pallets and the nursery was a large place, or so we thought.

One day Brad and I were sitting on some pallets inside our little hideout when the foreman came in. He looked down at us and said, "I know it's not your fault there are no pallets to be emptied, but we can't use you two anymore. Come into the office and I'll give you your checks."

So much for the part-time job. But it was still early, so we decided to go snorkeling by Palos Verdes because it made no sense to waste a good day.

Golden Brick Road

The weather was hot that year in California, and the whole family was looking forward to a vacation. Dad had just polished the car, changed the oil, and did some maintenance on the engine of his 1955 Cadillac. He placed a luggage rack on top of the roof and had all our camping gear packed and ready to go. We lived in Long Beach, California and we were headed for Yosemite, so it would take some time to get to where we were going. Yosemite National Park was just one of the National Parks I remember going to when I was younger.

I was looking forward to seeing those giant redwood trees that you could drive a bus through, not to mention the fishing, hiking, exploring, outdoor cooking, and girl watching in the neighboring camps, beside an open campfire, which I just loved.

So there we all were: my Mom, the best cook in the world; Dad, who is really my step-dad, but he was the only father I knew since my real dad ran away when I was three years old; my sister, Paulette, who was 4 years younger than me, and who all my boy friends wanted to meet; and my baby half-brother, Willis, who seemed to always have things coming out one end or the other. "Going to be a cool head, when he grows up." I had that written on a picture of him that I carried around with me all the time. Meaning that he was alright, he was my brother. That's the way we talked back then. Ooh yes! Cindy the dog was with us too, a black Cocker Spaniel, Dad's main friend when the rest of us weren't around. That day though, we were off together, not to see the wizard, but to have some good wilderness adventures.

Becoming A Man

I joined the United States Air Force on 30 September, 1959, in Downey, California, and had to have my parents' permission because I was only seventeen years old. I believe they were glad to see me go.

My step-dad had to go before a judge because of some things that had happened just before I left for the service, which had to do with a friend of mine named Roy. Roy ran away from home because of an abusive father. His father would beat him with a belt all over his body, sometimes using the buckle end of the belt. After Roy ran away, his father called the police to find him, suggesting my house. The police broke into my house like gangbusters because Roy was staying with me. Roy had come to me for help and needed a place to stay. Isn't that what friends are for? To make matters worse, while staying at my house, Roy stole some pain pills from my step-dad who used them for relief from his tooth surgery. When the police broke in, Roy was caught locked in our bathroom, trying to flush the pills down the toilet. It frightened Mom to death because the police didn't knock, they just broke the front door, and they also came in through the windows, front and back. A court date was set for a hearing on the matter, but I was due to be in basic training before then. I left two weeks before the hearing, by train, to begin my Air Force career, so Bill, my step-dad, appeared in court and convinced them to let me remain in the service. He has always stood in my corner, as a good father should. My real father ran away from the family when I was three years old, and Bill will always be "Dad" to me. Roy was returned to his father's house and I never heard from him again.

My first military assignment, like all the young men and women going into the Air Force, was at Lackland Air Force Base, just outside of San Antonio, Texas. "Basic Training" was the first stop to see if you could make it as a military man or woman. There they teach you how to dress, shave, cut your hair, make your bed, shine your shoes, follow orders, and a lot more if you make it that far. After six weeks of "boot camp," as my Dad calls it, and if you hadn't been sent back home to your mother, as many were, you got your first stripe, or promotion to Airman Third Class. Then you received either an assignment to a technical school for further training, or a permanent duty station and on-the-job training. I was directed to go to Malmstrom Air Force Base, in Montana. There I entered into the commercial transportation squadron to begin my career in the transportation field. I loaded and unloaded airplanes, trains, trucks and anything else with people and cargo, or "traffic" as it is referred to in that career field.

I made it through the six weeks of basic training and was allowed to take leave before going to my new duty station. I didn't want to go home yet, and I had made a new friend named Tom. He wanted me to come home with him to Dayton, Ohio, hang out a

70

couple of weeks, and then go up to Malmstrom Air Force Base, which is outside of Great Falls, Montana. This is what I decided to do.

Traveling by train to Dayton, Ohio, we met two other Airmen, and we all began to harmonize the song" Down By the Riverside." We sounded pretty good, so we told these girls we'd met on the train that we were in a singing group going to Chicago to make a record. We didn't want them to think we were just out of basic training, especially since our hair had grown back. They believed us, and we got to know them a lot better. I enjoyed our time together, chasing women, home cooking, and reminiscing about basic training. Tom's family was very nice and accommodating, treating me just like a son, but I was getting anxious to catch a train to Great Falls to see what Montana had to offer. After two weeks, I said my good-byes and was off to Montana.

I arrived in Great Falls on the evening train wearing my uniform and a heavy wool topcoat. The air seemed dry, but cold, and my breath was always before me. Snow was on the ground, and a strong wind whipped around the train station. The steam came up and out from under the train, and the conductor called, "all aboard," as the train began to pull out. As I walked into the train station, it gave me the feeling of déjà vu, or maybe reminded me of a movie I had seen.

I realized then that I was on my own, only seventeen, in a town where I knew nobody and nobody knew me, more than three thousand miles away from home. I wasn't sure what to do next. Inside the station I found a phone on the wall next to a very faint, faded sign that read, "Incoming personnel to Malmstrom call:" and

71

then it gave a phone number. I called the number and a guy on the other end of the phone said he would send a car for me in about forty-five minutes. I asked him how Great Falls was, and he told me that if I looked out the window I would see the tallest building in town. I didn't even have to look up. It was a hotel, maybe five stories high. The rest of the buildings looked like bars. I later found out there were about two hundred and forty of them in that area. The next surprise I got was when I bought a candy bar. I handed the clerk a twenty dollar bill for a candy bar and newspaper, and he handed me back nineteen silver dollars and some change. Come to find out, they didn't have any paper one dollar bills in Montana in 1959 and 1960, only silver. Wish I would have saved some.

A military station wagon finally arrived at the train station and picked me up. After a thirty minute ride, we were outside the city and I noticed at the end of this long four-lane road we were on, a building in the middle of the road with a large sign on the top which read, "Welcome to Malmstrom Air Force Base." We slowed down, preparing to stop, but still doing around forty-five miles per hour when I noticed a piece of paper pass us; the wind was strong. The land was barren and the wind didn't seem to let up. It was mixed with a little snow. We stopped at the building in the center of the road and a guard came out in a parka, or arctic jacket and asked for my identification. So this was going to be home for the next whatever?

Becoming A Veteran

I had mixed feelings about going to Vietnam. I spent most of my four years at Great Falls, Montana, and now they were shipping me to Vietnam for my last year of duty in the United States Air Force. I wanted to go overseas because I had never been, but people were getting killed in "Nam," which is what we all called it. For some reason I wasn't that afraid of dying, and I heard you got your base of choice when you pulled a tour there. Besides, I was thinking about staying in the service.

I remember my step-dad, Bill, saying at the dinner table, "If I had stayed in the service, I would have been retired by now." I have always looked up to him, though he would never have known it as rebellious as I had been. He only had an eighth grade education, but he was as smart as anyone I knew. He could fix anything. Little kids used to bring their broken toys and leave them on our front porch in Long Beach, California. He would fix them and place them back on the porch, and they would be gone the next day. I guess God places people like that to help kids that don't have a father to fix their broken toys. I know He placed him in our family after my biological father ran away when I was three years old. So his advice was always considered in my mind.

Anyway, I didn't have a choice about going to Vietnam. I flew from Travis Air Force Base, California to Honolulu, Hawaii, then to Guam, and then to Clark Air Base in the Philippines where I spent the night. Then I flew the next day to Ton Son Nhut Air Base, Vietnam. One of the things I remember most about that trip was how, at Travis Air Force Base, I felt lost among so many people in all services heading all over the world. I felt like the character Waldo in today's scenario of "Where is Waldo?" At Honolulu, Hawaii, I remember getting off the aircraft while it was being refueled, smelling the Jasmine flowers in the air, and thinking what a wonderful place it must be to live in. Guam was just another island, but it did have beautiful water around it. So many shades of green and blue inviting you to take a swim. By the time I arrived in the Philippines, I had made some friends and we all went to the airmen's club on Clark Air Base. That had to be the best airmen's club in the South Pacific: good food, cheap drinks, lots of women, and a marvelous band. After tying one on, which means "getting drunk" for those who don't drink; we had breakfast at the airmen's club in the morning and then boarded our flight for Ton Son Nhut.

There were plenty of things I had to get used to during my tour in Vietnam, beginning with the temperature. It was so hot and muggy, I was soaked by the time I left the plane and before I was

74

inside the air terminal. There was no air conditioning either, only large fans. It took me some time to adjust. The air was so moist it was like being in a steam bath.

Another thing that took getting used to was taking showers and shaving in cold water, not to mention what you may find in your shower. We lived in tents when I first got over there, and the showers were outside surrounded by wooden planks. I would wrap a towel around myself, grab my soap, toothbrush and toothpaste, and head for the showers in the morning. One airman did exactly the same thing one morning, and to his surprise, there was a twelve-foot python lying in the corner of the shower. The airman forgot his towel and ran through the camp naked. We thought Vietnam had gotten to him until others reported the snake. Some army troops killed the snake and hung it up on the barbed wire fence we had around the compound.

Next, I never saw so many different kinds of bugs as I saw in Vietnam. There were beetles over there the size of small turtles. Sometimes we would ride to work on the back of a pickup truck in the morning, or hitch a ride to the tent compound in the evening. One day an airman stood up, facing forward while the truck was moving, and this flying beetle hit him right in the chest, almost knocking him out of the truck, and cracking a couple of his ribs. Fortunately the truck had only been going about fifteen miles per hour. He never stood up in the truck again.

Then there were the mosquitoes. We had to sleep under mosquito nets or get eaten by mosquitoes. One airman came in drunk one night and didn't use his net. In the morning he looked like he had the measles. I felt sorry for him.

There were monsoon seasons over there where the rains came down so hard you could hold your hand out in front of yourself and barely be able to see it. Also, the wind blew so hard sometimes that the torrential rain became horizontal and almost cut into you.

There were also some good things about living there. We all had what they called "house girls." They should have called them, "tent girls." For five dollars they would wash and iron our clothes, make our beds, and shine our shoes for the week.

Anyway, I was assigned to the 8th Aerial Port Squadron where I worked in the Air Terminal manifesting, channeling, packing, loading and unloading passengers and cargo for shipment in and out of the base.

The Day President Kennedy Was Shot

I was in Saigon, Vietnam the day it happened. Actually, it was night time for me. I had just reenlisted for another four years of active duty in the United States Air Force, and I was celebrating with champagne and cheese sandwiches. Champagne mostly, the sandwiches were just an attempt to keep me from getting too drunk. I couldn't get any hors d'oeuvres or finger sandwiches to go with the champagne; besides, I didn't want to get too fancy since it was just another four years out of my life. But when I heard the news about President Kennedy being shot, I didn't need the sandwiches or the champagne for that matter.

I wondered what was going to happen. I remember talking to an army police patrol that was making the rounds in Saigon. They told me the president had just been shot, and that I needed to return to my unit at Ton Son Nhut Air Base, Vietnam.

I had heard that the F.B.I. didn't care for the president, but I liked him and voted for him. I thought he had class for a politician and was good for America. I remember that he stood down the Russian missiles to Cuba with a naval blockade, which put our unit on full alert, and we were ready for any action that might have

77

occurred. I was stationed at Malmstrom Air force Base, Montana then, where some of the Minuteman missile complexes were placed. I know because I helped bring in the equipment for the complexes. And if missiles started flying, these would be the first.

After talking to the army police patrol, I was sober and I hailed down a sickle low boy, which was the cheapest form of transportation, (a bicycle with a seat in front to carry passengers) and I returned to the base, still not knowing just what would happen now that I had reenlisted for another four years.

Saigon, Vietnam

I remember a time when I was living on Todo Street in Saigon, Vietnam with a Vietnamese girl named Lai. I met Lai in a bar one night and we started dating, and after a while I moved in with her. Living with her was a lot nicer than living in the barracks on the base that I was assigned to, and it took my mind off of what was going on around me. We had just gotten over a Cholera epidemic in the country and one day I was watching a demonstration outside of Lai's upstairs terrace window, which overlooked Todo Street.

There was a Buddhist monk clothed in a bright orange robe and there were many Vietnamese people crowded all around him. There were also three or four more monks standing in a line at the front of the crowd. The monk sat down in the middle of the street, and one Vietnamese man came forward from the crowd and poured gasoline over him from a 5 gallon can. The people stood back as the monk took out a lighter and set himself on fire. He didn't scream or make any kind of noise, he just sat there on fire until the flames had blackened him and he finally fell over. He continued to burn as the crowd shouted in Vietnamese and waved banners of white with red letters. Then the police started to arrive and arrest people. They were trying to gain control over anyone they could catch. I went back inside from the small window terrace and waited until it was all over so I could go back to the base. Lai told me they were demonstrating because the police were arresting people and torturing them to try and get information about who didn't support the Ngo Dinh Deim government, who sided with the Viet Cong, or who just didn't like Madame Ngo Dinh Nhu, the President's brother's wife. It was reported that she tortured people just for kicks.

Later that year the military overthrew the Deim government, but Madame Nhu escaped to France. I was told she was even worse than President Deim. They caught him trying to escape with a briefcase full of American dollars, and he was shot by the military along with his brother, Madame Nhu's husband. People tore down statues of Madame Nhu and tried to start a new government. While this battle was going on, I sat with the rest of my buddies in the yard of our new barracks at Ton Son Nhut, Air Base. We watched planes from the nearby airport take off to fly over Saigon and fire rockets down at the Vietnamese naval ships in the harbor. They would then go back to the airport, load more rockets on their planes, and repeat the attack. I was told the Vietnamese Air Force and Army were fighting the Vietnamese Navy and Marines. Each time the Air Force planes fired their rockets and hit their targets, they did a victory roll with their planes and then flew back for more rockets. The "ack, ack" shell bursts exploded all around the aircraft as it did its dive into the harbor. It reminded me of a World War II movie with the shell shots from the ships exploding around the propeller driven aircraft. I never did see a plane get shot down though, so I guess the Air Force was winning.

 All the American troops were restricted to the base, so we all sat in the yard by our barracks, drinking beer and watching the planes dive on the harbor where the ships were. Some of the guys came back from town telling stories of being shot at with machine guns in the zoo, and seeing animals and people get shot there also. They said they had to scale a 10 foot wall with broken glass on top of it to get out of the zoo, but when the Vietnamese military started shooting at them, the wall was no problem. Others said they saw our servicemen staggering in and out of bars on Todo Street as people fought and fired guns in the streets. I had come in from Saigon in a sickle low, which is a bicycle with a seat for passengers on the front—a poor man's taxi. The sickle lows had plastic covers on them in case of rain. I pulled the cover over the front so no one could see who I was, in case the Viet Cong were looking for Americans in all the chaos around me. When we got to the main gate of Ton Son Nhut, Air Base, there was an army tank in front with many armed guards around it. As we pulled up to the gate, the commander of the tank slowly aimed the barrel of the tank's gun down at the sickle low that I was in which made me a little nervous. After I pulled back the plastic cover and they saw it was an American serviceman they let me pass by and return to my unit on base.

A Life In My Hands

After spending a year in Vietnam, I was reassigned to Tachikawa Air Base, Japan. I was 21 years old, away from home, and making it on my own.

In Vietnam, besides learning how to kill and not be killed, I learned how to drink, run women, and act big. Now, stationed in Japan, I continued this lifestyle, and found a nice little Japanese girl to live with named Yoshiko. Yoshiko is a common name in Japan.

Yoshiko came from a very wealthy family who owned a sake factory and a large amount of a major car company in Japan. It was their tradition to arrange a marriage for their daughter with another family. But like me, Yoshiko had gone away from family tradition and started dating outside of her family's wishes. We lived together for two years and had talked about marriage, but I thought that bringing a Japanese wife home would not go over very well with my family, and that the society I lived in did not look favorably on mixed marriages. If we married, Yoshiko would be far away from home, living among people looking down on her. Neither of us would have wanted that.

While living together, we had sex all the time, and she became pregnant more than once. We had the child aborted each time, and this is the worst regret in my life. I left Japan in 1964, never to return to Yoshiko. I had asked her once what she would do if we never got married. She said she would return to her family. May God, Yoshiko, and my unborn children forgive me.

Yoshiko and I in Kobe, Japan

Dads Are Wonderful!

Leta
Vern
Reineke

After one year at Ton Son Nhut Air Base, Vietnam and two years at Yokota Air Base, Japan, I had finally returned to the good old United States of America. In April 1966, I was stationed at Shaw Air Force Base, South Carolina—Southern cooking, big-eyed girls and English speaking people. The swamps of Santee Cooper around Sumter, South Carolina, the town outside of the base, had the best hunting and fishing around. I was only one hundred miles from Myrtle Beach, South Carolina so partying, eating, and drinking, were all in my mind's eye. It was good to be home.

My mother and step-dad lived in Hagerstown, Maryland, along with other family members, and I could take leave and visit them quite often. It was only five hundred and fifty miles, or ten hours travel time.

Shaw Air Force Base was a tactical base which mobilized quite often for the deployment and support of fighter aircraft. I was in charge of the air terminal, making sure everything went according to plans written from specs from higher headquarters and put into practice by the base. The tactical units would send me a copy of their shipping requirements in advance, and I would tell them how to ship it: by air, the type of packing to use, how to properly label and handle it, etc. When they deployed, I would manifest and load their equipment and personnel onboard cargo carrying aircraft, planning the load arrangements in advance of deployment. Sometimes we would almost ship out the entire base.

My first trip was up to see Mom and my step-dad, Bill. My biological father ran away when I was only three, and I considered Bill to be my real Dad because he had always been there for me. As a matter of fact, during that trip he told me that he had bought my sister a car, and that he wanted to be fair with me and buy me one too, treating all us kids alike. Dads are wonderful!

We went out to this farmhouse that belonged to a farmer that Dad knew, and there, sitting behind the barn in tall grass was a 1955 Chevrolet with two doors and a six cylinder engine. It looked pea green with a bent bumper and torn seats, and the farmer wanted four hundred dollars for it. A 1955 Chevy! I knew the girls would go mad. Dad asked me if I liked it and I nonchalantly said, "yes", not wanting to seem too overjoyed in front of the farmer. Dad gave him the money and I drove it to Mom and Dad's house; I was in love.

This was the first real car I had ever owned. I had been overseas and didn't need a car and I couldn't afford a car while stationed in Montana, but Sumter, South Carolina was a place where you cruised the drive-in during the evenings and went to the beach on the weekends. Anybody that was anybody had a cool car and I was about to make the grade.

I borrowed Dad's car wax and began to wash and polish. The more I polished, the lighter the paint got until it was a robin's egg blue, beautiful. I would never have guessed the real color of the car from pea green to heavenly blue.

The next day Dad and I went to the junk yard and bought a bumper and radio for the car. I also rummaged an antenna for the radio and hubcaps, because I didn't like the ones that came on my car, and a chrome strip that was missing. Dad likes to work on cars, and he and I put the new bumper on and installed the radio. We then went to Western Auto and bought new blue and white seat covers that matched the color of the car. Finally, Dad tuned the engine, changed the oil, and checked the brakes, replacing those in the front. Then he took it to the gas station for a lube job, also filling the gas tank. Dads are wonderful!

I drove it back to Sumter, South Carolina and felt like every eye was watching me, envying my new car. When it went into passing gear and the power glide transmission cut in, forcing me back into my seat, I felt like I was flying. I thought to myself, it doesn't get any better than this. I drove that car until the cam shaft wore round, and still sold it for more than Dad had paid for it. Yes, he couldn't have bought me anything I wanted more. Dads are wonderful!

A Story I'm Glad I Can Tell

This story took place as Gayle and I were coming back from her mom and dad's farm in Chapel Hill, North Carolina. They owned about one hundred and forty-five acres there where they raised chickens and some livestock. We would sometimes go visiting them on Friday evenings after I got off of work at the air terminal on Shaw Air Force Base, South Carolina. I had been stationed there for almost two years, and I had just gotten married to Gayle.

I met Gayle at Myrtle Beach, which was about one hundred miles away from the base. She had ditched school with some of her girlfriends that day, and I had taken off from work and gone to the beach with my friend.

At the beach I used to pose as a photographer, shooting pictures that you could view on a key chain. That usually got me most girls' names, and if they wanted the pictures, I'd also get the hotel room they were staying at. I always had a friend that could go out with any of their girlfriends, because usually they never wanted to go out alone on the first date. All I had to do was take the pictures to a place around the corner. There was a little shop there that quickly developed the pictures and placed the positive/negative in a key ring holder. I made a profit for myself and got a date with the girl; it worked most of the time. Of course, I only took pictures of the girls I wanted to date.

Anyway, I got Gayle's address, phone number and an invitation to come up and see her in Chapel Hill. She was very photogenic, and I started going up to Chapel Hill each weekend to see her. Finally I asked her to marry me, after kind of being forced by her parents, but that's another story. We got married in a Baptist church near her mom and dad's farm, honeymooning no other place than Myrtle Beach.

Getting back to my story, it was Sunday evening around 11:30 p.m. and I was getting a little tired of driving. I was glad we were right outside of Sumter, South Carolina on route 15; another twenty minutes and we would be back home where I could get some sleep since I had to go to work in the morning. I enjoyed driving my new car, a Chevrolet Nova Super Sport. It had chrome wheels, a 327 cubic inch V8 engine, posit traction, rear suspension, with four on the floor stick shift transmission, and was painted fire engine red for notice. It also had the best wax job I could give it, and it was the first new car the bank and I had ever owned.

Route 15 into Sumter was a two lane highway with a twenty foot drop off into the swamp on both sides, and at this time of night there was hardly any traffic. I was doing about 65 miles per hour when I saw a car coming from the other direction traveling in the middle of the road. I slowed down a little and moved closer to the shoulder on my side, hoping this guy wasn't sleeping behind the wheel. The closer we got to each other, the more he came over on my side of the road. I then slowed down to about thirty miles per hour and was driving on the shoulder of the road when he sideswiped me. He never even slowed down a bit but sped up and kept on going.

After the momentary shock wore off, because I couldn't believe he hit me and kept on going, I shifted into second gear and did a 180 degree turn in the middle of the road just in time to see him turn left about a mile down the road. Smoke was pouring out from under my tires and my tachometer was starting to red line. I shifted into third gear coming up on the road he had turned on, fish tailing around the corner. My foot was on the floorboard as I neared the top of the small hill I had just seen him go over. I hit the top of the hill doing seventy five miles per hour and went airborne for a second, but he was still pouring it on heading down the road. When I hit the pavement coming over the hill, I shifted to fourth gear, double clutching so as not to miss the gear.

Gayle started crying because she didn't know what damage he had done to our car and she wasn't used to the way I was driving. To get her mind off what was happening I told her to get out a pencil and paper and write down the license number when I got close enough to his bumper. He wasn't going to get away with hitting my new car; he could have knocked us into the swamp and killed both of us. I was doing over a hundred miles per hour when I finally caught up to him. He slowed down to about ninety because of the road being so curvy and hilly, but never did stop. Gayle was still crying, but she managed to write down the license number, then I slowed down and stopped, but he kept on going.

After catching my breath, I turned around, headed to a country bar a couple miles back, and stopped to call the police. They identified the owner of the license plate, and when they went to his residence his car was parked in the driveway with red paint all over the side of it. They got him up out of bed and questioned him, finding him drunk with no memory of what had happened.

My new Nova Super Sport needed a new bumper, front quarter panel, and door, but we were lucky the guy only sideswiped us. I believe the good Lord was watching over us that night, or this story would have never been told; not by me anyway.

A Boat Ride

When I was assigned to the Commercial Transportation Section in the Transportation Squadron on Shaw Air Force Base, South Carolina, Danny Bowman and Bud Youmans were head of the air terminal on base. Their Air Force specialty code (A.F.S.C.) put them in the transportation career field and assigned them to the Transportation Squadron. They used to drive a locomotive engine back and forth between Sumter, South Carolina and Shaw Air Force Base, picking up freight cars for the base, plus doing other little odds and ends as needed for the squadron. My specialty was air transportation, but both Danny and Bud out ranked me, so even though it was my specialty, they wrote my performance report and I worked for them.

Bud Youmans has become a very good friend of mine since I first met him. He was an outdoors person and now is retired from the Air Force and from being game warden for the state of South Carolina. A native of South Carolina, he taught me to hunt and fish in the swamps of the Santee River area which is one of the best places in the United States for these sports.

When I arrived in South Carolina, I did very

little hunting or fishing, but after getting married to Gayle we bought a new 14 foot tri-hall McKee craft, with a 45 hp Evinrule motor, short shift, and a new tilt trailer, plus a gun collection any hunter would be proud of. The boat and motor could be used for skiing and Gayle and I liked to go up to the lake with some friends when we had the chance. You could rent a cabin from the base for next to nothing. But for fishing I carried a little three and half horse power boat motor with a collapsible shaft in a case in my trunk, to use on john boats. The best fishing was for catfish and landlocked rock fish that weighed up to fifty pounds and were in the river. This is what I used the new McKee craft for. I would anchor in the middle of the river, front and back, to keep the boat straight, then place two poles out the back letting the current carry the bait down stream. These saltwater rock bass had swam up river and were trapped or stopped from returning to the ocean by man-made dams that were built to produce electrical power for the area, also to provide man-made lakes and swamp areas for wildlife.. And they began to reproduce, making a fantastic freshwater sport fish in the river. But for sun fish, and small and large mouth bass, we went to the swamps in aluminum and wooden flat bottom boats called john boats.

One summer Gayle and I went camping by a lake that was near the swamp. We were out skiing when I spotted this aluminum john boat with a young couple and an elderly lady waving at us. I went over to see what was wrong and they had run out of gas. They had been fishing for sun fish and bass using crickets and worms for bait, but not having too much success. When they decided to return to their camp they found out they had used up all their gas. It just wasn't their day. I had never towed anyone before, but I didn't think it would be any trouble so I threw them a line and told them to tie it off in their boat. I started out slow with Gayle in the back of our boat watching. The girl was up front in their boat where the rope was tied, and her husband was by the engine in the back of their boat. Their mother or grandmother, I don't know which, was in the middle holding on to both sides of their boat with cricket pots by her feet and fishing poles in the boat between her legs. She looked kind of funny with a large rim straw hat on and a homemade dress from the fifties. Everyone else had shorts and tee shirts. Anyway, I started to go a little faster and their boat kept going back and forth between my wakes but everything seemed to be working ok. So I sped up to about half throttle and I heard Gayle holler. I turned around just in time to see their flat bottom boat do a complete flip in mid air. The girl was thrown out the front and the guy went out the back of their boat. The boat landed right side up again and I throttled all the way back and came to a complete stop. I looked again and that poor old lady was still holding on to both sides of their boat. Crickets were crawling all over her face and her hat had taken a bath but was still on her head. She was soaking wet with her hair all in front of her face, and she wasn't saying a word. I picked up the girl and her husband in my boat, and when I went to put the old lady in my boat she said, "If I ever get on shore again, I will never get into another boat." I took them back to their camp with their boat tagging along behind me very slowly. I apologized a couple of times and went to our camp. But to this day I can still see that little old lady holding on to that boat for dear life. God bless her!

94

This is one of the safest boats on the river. You can walk around the edges of this boat without tipping it over. It's just the driver you have to watch out for.

A Fish Tale

Snorkeling is one of my favorite pastimes, and while stationed at Anderson Air Force Base, Guam, I acquired quite a seashell collection. I remember one day when Randy, Paul and I went snorkeling around a bomb crater located inside Guam's coral reef by the navy base on the south side of the island. I don't know whether it was the Japanese, Americans or Australians that dropped the bomb that made the crater, but it was a nice diving spot for snorkelers like us who were seeking seashells.

The water around Guam is so crystal clear that you can see about 500 feet under water on a good day. The abundance of tropical fish and live coral makes diving on Guam a sport unmatched, except maybe for the diving off of Australia's Great Barrier Reef, which is considered the best in the world. I have found Map Cowries though, that do not exist anywhere else except in Guam's United States Navy harbor, where the ships come in. They are about one-third the size of regular Map Cowries, and I have four of them in my seashell collection.

While we were snorkeling for shells one day a navy patrol boat was sent to pick us up in the harbor. They took us for a ride in their paddy wagon to the base security office. We were told that the area where we were shelling was off limits to unauthorized personnel, I guess because of the submarines that are in the harbor. Anyway, I got to keep the shells.

Getting back to my story, Randy, Paul and I were about one hundred yards offshore, swimming on top of the water and looking down at the sand trails. When we saw a trail in the sand, we swam down to the end of it and dug up whatever made the trail, which was usually a seashell. We then placed the shells in net bags that hung from our sides. The water was only about twenty feet deep, and swimming to the bottom was no problem. Not too many people came out that far, so the shelling was great. The coral changed as we swam out toward the end of the reef, which was about two hundred yards offshore, and with each change, we found different types of shells. Cowries hide among the Antler Coral, which is light pink in color with white tips, looking like horns on a deer. Razor Coral is fluorescent in color, and Cowries just love to hide under it searching for food. The shells we were looking for then were trumpets and olives and they come in all sizes and colors.

Soon, however, our attention switched abruptly from shells to something else. I was the first to see it, and it stopped me cold. Looking up at me with its mouth open and two large teeth hanging down, about the size of two forty-ounce coke bottles, was a Great

Barracuda. Those teeth were so big I almost didn't notice the
smaller ones running along the jawbone. It was about six to eight feet
long, swimming a couple of feet off the bottom, and looking straight at
us. Sideways it looked as big as two telephone poles; but then, water
tends to magnify things. It had one eye the size of a dinner plate that
was trained on us. The face was one-third of the total fish, with the
mouth and its two large teeth being two-thirds of the face. The body
was one-third and the tail was one-third. We had nowhere to go, and
there was nothing stopping it from making a meal of us, considering
that it was the fastest fish in the ocean.

Looking for support, I called to Paul and pointed down
to the fish. The fish stayed where it was, waving its body a little to
maintain its position. Paul began trying to cover up his shell net
because of the shiny metal handle. Barracudas have been known to
strike shiny objects, and Paul wasn't going to take any chances.
Meanwhile, Randy, unaware of the fish, swam on by us until he saw
it, and then I never saw anyone move as fast as he did trying to swim
back to the beach. We were still in trouble; if this fish wanted us, there
was nothing we could do to stop it. Paul and I just looked at it for
about a minute, and then the fish slowly moved away from us and out
of sight. We swam back to shore, looking all the way for our friend,
and no longer looking for shells.

I talked to other people on Guam and they too had seen
this creature of the deep. People started seeing it about three years
before we spotted it. So far, no one had been hurt by it, and it always
seemed to be around that bomb crater.

Talofofo Falls

Larry Perry, his wife Frieda, and Gayle and I decided to hike through the jungles of Guam to Talofofo Falls, the only freshwater swimming hole on the island. The girls packed a lunch and Larry and I gathered the equipment we would need: backpacks, machetes, ropes, insect repellent, knives, cameras, etc. We put on our bathing suits under our Levis because Talofofo Falls had a small lake at the bottom where we could take a swim and have a picnic. It would be an all day trip, but we would be back by evening.

Not that many people go to the falls. First of all, few know about it, and secondly, cutting your way through the vegetation, forging streams, and fighting insects is not everyone's cup of tea. But it sounded like fun to us, so off we went to the jungle to begin another adventure.

After parking our car at the beginning of the trail to the falls and dowsing ourselves with insect repellent, as shown on the left, I took the lead with my machete in hand. Fortunately, the only snakes on Guam were those that had come in on visiting ships that had docked at the island. As I hacked through the vegetation I thought about how easy it was to cut through the thick green leafs that hung down and covered the path in front

99

of me. A trail was there that had been covered by growing vegetation, but the machete sliced right through it with little effort on my part.

Finally we came upon a small stream where a raft was attached to a rope that ran across the water. The problem was that the raft had floated to the other side of the stream, the stream was twenty feet wide and three to four feet deep, and we needed to cross it to retrieve the raft. The water was partly covered with green moss, but I didn't think there were any piranhas or nasty things in the water, so in I went to fetch the raft. The water felt good after cutting my way through the jungle. I got the raft and took it back over to get Larry, Frieda, and Gayle.

We hiked another mile and came upon the bottom of the falls. We had to cross to the other side on large rocks in the water leading up to the falls; our goal was to get to the other side where a small beach and body of water were. After changing to our bathing suits we all took a dip in the small lake, stopping to take pictures and have lunch afterwards.

While exploring the area, I walked up under the falls and slipped off into the lake below, hitting my head on the ledge I had slipped off of, and getting a very bad cut on my forehead. We applied

100

pressure with a towel until the bleeding stopped, then wrapped a bandage around the top part of my head. All I needed was a feather to make me look like an Indian. After that we all headed back to the car with memories to take with us. I got three stitches to remind me to be more careful.

I was surprised at how heavy water can be hitting you on the top of your head from a waterfalls.

A Mount Fuji Helper

      I have a stick by my bed to help support me when my back gives out, as it sometimes does . The support I remember when I was younger leaves this body in pain and weakness if I sleep the wrong way or move too fast in the morning. So I depend on this stick, which I have had since the sixties, to help give me the support if I need it. It has many markings on it, which are brands, showing station numbers and altitudes. The story behind this is interesting.

      When I was in the Air Force and stationed on the island of Guam. I took an R and R (Rest and Relaxation) trip to Hong Kong, Okinawa, and mainland Japan with my first wife, Gayle, and our two close friends, Frieda and Larry. Arriving in

Tokyo, we decided to climb Mount Fuji. I was the only one that spoke Japanese so I set up the whole trip. We would climb Mount Fuji one day, spend the night on top of the mountain, and climb down the other side the next morning. After that we planned to spend that night in a native Japanese hotel and then take the monorail back to Tokyo the following morning.

Anyway, arriving in Tokyo and deciding to climb Mount Fuji, we took a subway train to a town near the mountain and then a cab to the main entrance of the trail that led to the top of Mount Fuji. There at the trail entrance, we each bought a "Fuji Pole" to help us climb the mountain. As we climbed, we stopped at different rest houses along the way where we were able to get energy drinks, green tea, and rice cakes or other snacks. We also had our Fuji Poles stamped, or branded, with the station number and the altitude we were at, to show we had made it that far.

At the very top of the mountain was a Buddhist Temple. The monks had a special seal or stamp they placed at the very top of the Fuji poles to show that we had made it to the top. They gave us their blessing, after a small donation of course, as proof of our visit to the shrine.

Each of these stamps or brandings cost us about 20 yen, or 7 cents, back then. We sat around a table with a heater or hot coals under the table, which was also covered with a blanket, while the caretaker branded our sticks, (Fuji poles). We drank tea and got our feet warm. Neat stuff huh? This was like setting it in stone that we were there.

There were close to forty-five stations along the way. At the first seven stations, we rode on horses, with the owner of the horse hanging on to the tail and being pulled up the mountain along with us. Poor horse! But after that, we were on our own (feet that is). As we climbed, the air got thinner and thinner and we had to stop every ten steps to rest and catch our breath. This is when our Fuji poles came in handy, supporting us as we continued up the mountain. We could look out and see clouds and airplanes flying beneath us. When we neared the top, the sun was starting to set and the sky was alive with color. The air felt cold and virginal, unlike anything I could imagine, so clean and pure.

When we got to the top of the mountain, there was a row of tin shacks with rocks on top of their tin roofs keeping the wind from blowing them away. We were all cold and dead tired, and I saw one shack with a dim light on. I knocked on a grass door and it slid open, revealing thirty or forty people in sleeping bags and blankets lying on the floor. We literally fell in the door and were sound asleep within minutes. We slept on the floor with all these people we didn't know, and they gave us some blankets to cover us. In the morning I woke up to the smell of green tea and fried fish. The air was cold, and I could see my breath as I took my head out from under the covers. Some Japanese men were cooking over a small fire in the middle of the room and talking about something I couldn't understand. I said "good morning" in Japanese and they smiled, bowed, and returned the greeting, offering me something to eat. I told them I'd like some tea and thanked them for their hospitality. I think that because it was so cold, my wife and our friends were waiting for everyone else to get up

104

before they would move. So, being as I had gotten them into this, I got up, put on my coat—we had all slept in our clothes—and got the tea that was offered to me. I don't know what I enjoyed the most, the tea or the fire it was being heated on. After everyone was up and had breakfast (I skipped the fish), we all went outside to see what we had come up for: the sunrise.

There are some things in life that you cannot explain, and the sunrise from the top of a very high mountain is one of them. To say it was beautiful would be an understatement. Like all God's creations to view it for the first time causes emotions that you cannot describe to someone else. The blues, whites, gold, reds, pinks, browns, and every other color were there in perfect order. As I tried to take a picture of it, my finger stuck to the camera lens because of the cold, but at that moment I barely noticed the cold, only the approaching warmth of the sun. After getting our Fuji poles stamped and receiving our blessing, we walked over to the crater side of the mountain. Many people don't know that Mount Fuji is also a volcano which has erupted 16 times over the past century or so. This made the trip a little more exciting, knowing we were on top of an active volcano. We decided to look down inside, which was brave, but not too smart. Thank goodness, all I saw was a little steam coming up out of a large hole in the ground. We then decided to follow the plan and climb down the other side. In the back of my mind, I was hoping our luck would hold, and that the mountain wouldn't blow her top. After walking, sliding, and running down the other side of Mount Fuji, we hailed a cab and headed for our Japanese hotel where we left our shoes at the front door, enjoyed a in-house hot tub, ate with crop sticks, and were given a Japanese greeting, (welcome to Japan, won't you please come in?) And that's how I got the stick which now helps me when my back won't.

There were landscapes of clouds, topped with rainbows of color, as I looked from the top of Mount Fuji.

106

An Unhappy Christmas

It was about two weeks before Christmas and I was working grave shift at traffic control, Travis Air Force Base, California. I had just gotten to work and was arranging my console for the traffic we had scheduled that morning, when the zipper on my pants broke. I told my supervisor I needed to go home and change pants, and that it would only take an hour. I lived in Vacaville, California and the traffic was slow that time of night. He looked at the schedule and said, "Hurry back, I'll need you for this C-5 A coming in at 2:00 am." I told him I would be back way before then and I headed out the door.

The wind wasn't blowing like it usually does but it still was cold and damp. Christmas music was on the radio and some people still had their outside Christmas lights on even though it was after midnight. I always enjoyed the Christmas atmosphere. Arriving home around 12:45 am I expected my wife to be sound asleep, but the outside light was on and I could see the Christmas tree lights through the front window. I parked the car and went inside the house through the front door. I no sooner got inside when I saw

Gayle, my wife, standing in the bedroom doorway with a new black negligee on. I was thinking how nice it looked on her when I heard someone knocking on the front door. I turned around and opened the door to see a guy standing outside with a small blue present in his hand, but when he saw me he backed up and said, "I am sorry, I have the wrong house." Then he hurried back to a cab that was getting ready to pull away. With the front door still open I turned again toward the bedroom and looked at Gayle and said, "my zipper broke." She turned around, went back into the bedroom and went to bed. With heaviness in my stomach I went to the kitchen and got a drink of water from the sink. I then changed my pants and went back to work. I knew then, it was going to be an unhappy Christmas.

Pride Cometh Before A Fall

I still remember sitting on my new Yamaha 135 cc dirt bike, and looking out over the gravel pit at a large hill with a ten foot straight up elevation. I didn't have much experience at hill climbing. Hell! I had never ridden a motor bike before, except the one my girlfriend had in Vietnam, and even then, she did most of the driving with me on the back.

But I had just bought a beautiful candy apple red, five-speed dirt bike in Suisun, California, and I was determined to master it. Besides, how hard could it be? I had seen other people racing, hill climbing, doing wheelies, and looking cool; why not me?

My Yamaha had directional signals sticking out in back, with bright yellow lights at the end for right and left turns. Something you really don't need on a dirt bike, but for road traffic it was required, and nice to have. What I really liked were the candy apple red frame and fuel tank, decorated with white pin striping. She looked good, and I felt good sitting on her. Now to do a little hill climbing.

I started down a small incline, headed for my first real hill climbing experience. In first gear, I maxed the RPMs. (the engine's revolutions per minute). Shifting to second gear, I maxed the RPMs again. When I shifted to third gear and was nearing max RPMs, I hit the bottom of the hill and started up. Speed wasn't that important, but RPM's were everything. I leaned over the handlebars while still giving it gas, trying to place more weight on the front tire so the bike wouldn't flip over on me. The rear tire, or drive wheel, was bouncing around, hitting small holes, so I started looking for the best path to the top of the hill to avoid the bumps. The bike started losing RPMs, so I shifted to second gear. This put me back to max RPMs and gave the drive wheel the power to dig into the dirt and move the bike forward. When I hit the straight up incline of the hill, my nose was almost touching the front wheel. I don't know if I was praying, wishing, or just hoping, but I was up on top of the hill before I could finish. I stopped, looked back, and thought, "That wasn't too bad."

Well! if I did it once, I could do it again. No one was going to tell me it was just luck. Back to the bottom I went to practice my new found skill. I raced the engine's RPMs while sitting there at the bottom, looking back up at the hill again. Down the small incline I went, first gear, second gear, and third gear, hitting the bottom of the hill as before and starting up. Then for some reason, I thought to myself, "what if it was just luck?" Bad thought. I was at the beginning of the straight up incline and shifting to second gear when my RPMs began to go down. Then, right at the top the engine quit! When you're on the side of a cliff with no RPMs, there is no place to go but down.

Now, being as this was my first bike, I didn't want it to get messed up, so I tried to keep it from falling. Bad idea! You just don't hold back a 300 pound bike that has already started falling off of a cliff, especially if you're on the edge of the cliff with it! It could have been worse, though; I ended up with only torn clothes and scuffed up knees and arms. But the worst of it was that my new directional signals wouldn't be directing for some time. I lost a brake cable and a handgrip, and the candy apple red paint job wasn't nearly as flashy as before.

My pride had just been adjusted as I pushed my new bike back home.

My First Bachelor Pad

This new job was great, all I had to do was call in and see if there were any new trips to go on, and if not, I was free for the rest of the day. And even if there were trips, going on them was like going on a first class working vacation. Sure, I was responsible for an aircraft, a VC135/129, that I had to make sure was cleaned, equipped, and ready to go at all times, but when it was gone on a trip, my time was my own, and our aircraft was gone most of the time.

It was July, 1971, and I had been in the military for twelve years when I finally received my orders for the 89th Military Airlift Wing. It had taken a year to get my top secret clearance for this unit. I had volunteered for the job, which was at Andrews Air Force Base, while I was stationed on the other side of the country at Travis Air Force Base in California. I wanted to get away after resolving a very depressing divorce.

After receiving my orders, I drove from California, first to visit my mom and dad in Sandpoint, Idaho, taking a 30 day delay enroute for the visit. Then, across the United States I drove to my new duty station at Andrews Air Force Base, Maryland, home of the Presidential Squadron, the 89th Military Airlift Wing.

I was now on my own in a new city, with a new job, and my first real bachelor's apartment. The whole divorce thing had made me very depressed, but now things really seemed to be looking up. I found a two bedroom duplex at Carriage Hills Apartments complex in Silver Hill, Maryland, not too far from the base. The apartment

I rented was on the second floor and had a patio over-looking Suitland Parkway. It was a nice place just to sit and relax, with lots of trees to see, and not too much noise. The walkout patio was on the second floor, but my front door was a straight walk through from the parking lot and the front of the apartment building, which was on a hillside. I started fixing it up with items I collected on my travels with my new job. This was going to be my dream apartment, and with this job I had the whole world to shop in.

This fairly new apartment had just been repainted and had two bedrooms, a connecting living room and dining room, and a kitchen with a dishwasher, stove, refrigerator, and garbage disposal. It also had one walk-in closet between the two bedrooms, which were located down a small hallway on the left, past the dining room and kitchen. I turned the walk-in closet into a darkroom for film printing and developing, and equipped it with an enlarger, safe light, timer and a table with processing trays for film and prints. I kept my chemicals on a shelf in pharmaceutical bottles that I had gotten from the drug store. I needed a lab in my apartment because I had started shooting weddings and portraits part-time on the side. I did a lot of my own printing and developing because it was much quicker and cheaper than sending my work out to be processed.

The kitchen and dining room were separated by a wall, and there was an open archway between them. To my dismay the kitchen didn't have any windows. The dining room was lit by a hanging lamp with a large white globe surrounded by red and white glass flower petals. I had purchased it at an auction, and it hung over the dining room table and four white metal chairs that were covered in red leather. The table itself was also white metal with a black slate top.

I placed a round handmade brass serving tray on the northern wall. It was covered with a tin overlay to keep it from tarnishing. I had gotten this tray from Iran, and it was engraved with the twelve tribes of Israel, with Abraham and Moses in the center and the twelve tribes around the edge. The tray was round, along with a large round red throw rug I had under my round dining room table, and it matched the décor of this eating area.

The living room and dining room were connected by two large picture windows, one on each side of a wide sliding glass door on the eastern wall of the apartment. The sliding glass door led to the walkout patio. In the mornings, I could see the sunrise through the trees as I drank my coffee and ate the fresh doughnuts from the bakery just down the street. I wasn't too worried about my weight then, and one of the best ways out of depression is to enjoy some of life's little pleasures. I had semi-partitioned the living room and dining room with a portable stereo cabinet that was handmade for me in California. I could take it apart and configure it in different shapes depending on how I wanted to use it. It not only held my four-way Pioneer speaker system with fifteen inch woofers for bass, but also a Pioneer belt driven turntable, a Teac professional tape recorder, a large musical tape selection, a 21-inch color television set, a Sansui 180 Amp turner/amplifier, a telephone answering system, my bible reference book collection, and knickknacks that I had collected over the years.

All the furniture was contemporary, including my red, white, and blue plaid couch, and the original batik painting that hung over it, which I had gotten from Taiwan. I had two wood and glass tables in

front of the couch that were intended to be used as end tables, but with the limited space of the apartment, they served me better as coffee tables. Plus, I could walk between them and clean them easier that way. I had a contoured black fuzzy chair where I sometimes sat to play my 12 string Fender guitar and entertain my guests. Sometimes I used it for a backdrop when I photographed small kids.

I had a hanging scented candle that kept the smoke down to a pleasant smell, and autographed pictures on the wall of the White House and some of the people I had flown with. I had one photo of President Ronald Reagan who was Governor of California when

I first met him. Another painting, which came from Hong Kong, was a country scene with trees, flowers, and a small stream flowing toward the setting sun. The sun had just gone out of sight, but you still could see the reflection in the tree tops. It graced my western wall just inside the door of the apartment's entrance, and it was lit with an overhead light attached to the frame, creating a cool, peaceful mood, lazily leading your eyes toward the resting sun in the water.

I had white carpet in part of the apartment, black and white tile on the kitchen floor, medium blue carpet in the larger bedroom in the rear of the apartment, and just a plain wooden floor with grass mats in the smaller bedroom. Besides the round red carpet under the dining room table, I had another red carpet, made of the same material, covering most of the living room. It gave a three dimensional effect with the white carpet underneath. I had each carpet cut to fit the area where I wanted it, and I had them bound to keep them from fraying.

For the picture windows I bought red and white floor- to- ceiling drapes. They had six panels each and I had them sewn together, two red panels and two white panels, alternating them on a rod which ran above the picture windows and sliding glass door. I could open or close off the whole patio from the inside with a draw-string. They were also lined so I could keep the light out completely if I wanted, and so that no sunlight could fade the carpet and furniture.

There were twelve apartments in my building, and each had a lockable storage cage under the building where the laundry room was. In my storage cage I kept most of my storage containers for my electronic and photographic equipment.

Since it was a bachelor pad, I decided to decorate the bedrooms differently. One was decorated with a masculine approach, with animal skin throw rugs, and a real fur bedspread that I had picked up from overseas, and either satin sheets or four hundred thread cotton sheets. I tried silk sheets one time, but discovered that they wrinkle too much after they're washed. The room had windows on the northern and eastern walls, and the décor was mainly blue, white, and brown. I hung light blue sheer curtains with Venetian blinds underneath for privacy. I set up a drafting table against the eastern window. I needed the light when I sat there to oil paint my sepia tone photographs.

The other bedroom was more interesting; it was psychedelic in keeping with the flower children decor, including a waterbed, black lights, and hanging candles. I placed an old green wool army blanket over the windows, and I had fluorescent paint and brushes on a small table nearby so guests could paint their names, and whatever else they wanted, on the blanket that was lit up by a black light. I still have that blanket today, along with the memories of that room and the well wishes of my guests. I faced the waterbed toward the eastern double window so that anyone floating there could read what other guests had written or painted on the blanket.

There were different fluorescent posters on the walls, also lit by black lights which I had placed around the room, and I had incense to burn on the table. A small stereo and movie projector were on a stand next to the bed to provide entertainment for my guests. If they used the projector, they had to use the wall for a screen. I also had an assortment of movies for my guests to watch, as well as some homemade ones I had made of some of my trips. Instead of a door, I had glass beads hanging down over the doorway. On the ceiling I had multi-colored fabric draped down in parachute fashion, which created a kind of sultan's atmosphere. A multi-colored blanket was also fastened to the ceiling to make a hallway on the right side of the room from the doorway as you entered. This was both to prevent the black lights from being affected by the other lights in the apartment, and vise versa, and to hide the closet. On the bare floor, to keep everyone's feet from getting cold, I had grass mats. I guess I should have had slippers, but I did provide Japanese kimonos for my guests. Too bad there was no sunken tub in the bathroom, but sometimes you just have to make do.

To go along with my new apartment and new found freedom, I bought a fire engine red, Chevrolet Malibu convertible with a white top, denoting the good guy. I also became good friends with my mailman, Pat Jenkins, and he used to look after my apartment when I went on trips. I gave him a key, and he used to take breaks in my apartment during his mail run in the apartment complex. He was also the person who introduced me to my future second wife, Patsy, and even today he is still my best friend. But that's another story.

VC 135/129

     After being assigned to the 89th Military Airlift Wing (MAW) for about five years, I became a VC 135 flight instructor and was given my own aircraft to take charge of and maintain while it was at Andrews Air Force Base, Maryland.

     Although I flew on other aircraft, the VC 135, tail number 129, is the one I was responsible for with regard to what was put on it and how it was to be maintained. It was my job to ensure that it was mission ready at all times. This type of aircraft was designed for long distance travel, and the 89th MAW had five of them. The VC 135 has extra gas tanks in the belly, and I personally have flown on one of them from Tokyo, Japan, to Washington D.C. non stop, which took about thirteen and a half hours. During that flight we served two full meals plus a snack to the passengers and crew. It was a long day, but thankfully we didn't have days like that too often.

119

After returning home that day, we still had to clean the airplane and make it mission ready before we could go home and rest. That meant vacuuming the Distinguished Visitor compartment and making the beds, vacuuming the main cabin and refolding all the blankets, removing the disposable pillowcases from any used pillows, and vacuuming the crew compartment.

We also had to wipe down the interior walls of the entire aircraft, clean all the seats, dump and wash the ashtrays, remove the old headrest covers, remove any trash on the aircraft or anything left behind on any of the seats, and clean the bathrooms and restock them with new supplies such as: toothpaste, hairspray, aftershave, hand soap, cloth hand towels, etc. Additionally, we had to remove any soiled towels, sheets or blankets from the cabin and berthing area, and make sure that fleet service dumped the toilets and refilled them with clean water along with the galley's potable water so the plane would be ready for the next trip. Then we had to take our trashcan—a large rectangular metal box with a large plastic bag for a liner—and any other trash, along with our two metal coffee jugs and five metal two-gallon water jugs (that were used on the trip and were part of the aircraft's inventory) to Andrews' in-flight kitchen to be cleaned, sterilized, and returned for the next trip.

The galley also had to be cleaned which meant washing the floor, cleaning the ovens and removing any dry ice that we had used for refrigeration. There were tray carriers to be cleaned, dishes and silverware to be washed and made ready for the next flight, and we had to replace any cloth napkins and tablecloths we had used. We took any supplies we had brought for that trip off the plane, so the next

120

crew had room for their supplies, and we sprayed air freshener and laid down aisle runners as we walked off the plane.

It made for a very long day, but we knew we had given our very best and that we represented the United States of America, which gave us a satisfaction that only a job well done can give. I had also earned the title of Instructor in that career field, which made me very proud to be a part of the 89th Military Airlift Wing.

THE WHITE HOUSE
WASHINGTON

Best wishes from Richard Nixon

An Earthly Love

Riding a horse down a mountain at a forty-five degree angle may look easy on television, but when you're trying to look confident next to your new bride, it makes you feel a little anxious. Patsy Wood Dean, now Mrs. Fowler, my new bride, hollered at me, "look Gary, deer." There were about five deer, fifteen feet beside us, snacking on vegetation as they walked up the mountain as if we were a normal sight to them, having not a care in the world. They blended into the environment so well I would have missed them completely if it weren't for Patsy. This was our honeymoon trip in Yellowstone National Park and it was turning into some of the best days of my life.

After getting married in Southern Maryland, we traveled up to see my mom and dad in Sandpoint, Idaho, then on to Yellowstone National Park. But first we had stopped at the Wisconsin Dell's famous Paul Bunion Restaurant which provided trays of steak, chicken, fish, and half gallons of milk for us to eat and drink. Afterwards we rode on an amphibian duck through some of the most beautiful landscape cut into the wilderness by tannic waters in

122

Wisconsin. We also stopped at South Dakota's Bad-lands National Monument where I dug up a small wild cactus with a yellow flower on it, for a souvenir of our wedding, using a silver fifty cent piece which was the only digging tool I had. Traveling on to Oklahoma, we bought matching cowboy and cowgirl outfits, with real cowboy and cowgirl boots. We arrived at Mom and Dad's in Sandpoint, Idaho and enjoyed some trout fishing. Mom and Dad got to know Patsy a lot better and vise versa. Mom took Patsy shopping and Patsy baked Dad some cookies while we were there. We then headed back through Yellowstone's Northern exit and spent a night in a one room wooden cabin with a pot belly stove that got so hot it ran us out of the cabin that night. I had to cool it off with some water and remove some of the wood I had put into it. This started our adventures in Yellowstone which will live in my heart forever.

We had just seen a wolf track a wounded buck around a hill we were on, to a stream where the buck was resting. As the wolf advanced, the buck caught his scent, but since the buck's leg was hurt he stood his ground. The wolf, sensing the wound, advanced even closer until the buck lowered his head and charged with antlers down, trying to impale the wolf. The wolf gave ground and the buck charged again, showing the wolf this wasn't going to be an easy meal. Finally the buck and wolf ran out of sight and I still wonder what happened to that wounded buck. It did give me more respect for a wild deer and a wolf in that both were dangerous and not to be taken lightly.

By now I was trying my best not to fall out of the saddle and hoping this poor horse wouldn't lose his footing.

Our guide, and even Patsy looked like the picture on television, but believe me, it's not that easy. I felt like that cartoon cowboy who had just ridden his horse off of a cliff with both legs stretched out pulling back on the reins, and saying "whoa S.O.B., whoa!". However, we made it down to a level path on the mountain that led around a three foot ledge with a drop off of one half mile straight down. Again my thoughts were on the sure footedness of this animal I was riding. I remember how beautiful those mountains were and the grandeur of it all. Nature paints a picture that man can only admire and hope to maintain. But I still leaned toward the bank; not that I didn't trust the horse, but I just didn't want to be buried at the foot of this mountain, that's all. After that outing on horse back, our next stop was Old Faithful where we stayed at the Grand Lodge. It had fireplaces you could walk in and everything was made of wood, stone, and antlers. I got used to seeing large stuffed animals in the hotel all around, but when I was taking a picture of Old Faithful outside, I turned around to see this elk walking about twenty feet from me. His back was higher than my head and it was as if he didn't even know I was there. You can guess what my next picture was of. This was almost like scuba diving on Guam where the fish would come right up to you. I am surprised more people don't get hurt while exploring Yellowstone. We did see black bears on the side of the road, but the rangers advised us not to feed the bears or get out of our cars. Only pictures from the car were a good idea, and the bears needed to forage on their own. We saw lakes and waterfalls, and coming out of Yellowstone at the southern exit were the Grand Teton Mountains with snow on the top, a picture for any artist. My mind and senses were kept so busy on that trip that I stopped smoking.

The thing I love the most about Yellowstone National Park is April. My daughter was conceived on this trip and we named her April Ann. She is my only child, conceived when I was in love with her mother and nature. There is only one other love that compares with the love I found in Yellowstone and His name is Jesus.

It's too bad things don't last long in this life time.
The bible says all things will pass away and
all things will become new. But I believe
I will miss some of the old things.

A Father's Help

I only have one child. I would like to have had more, but it takes two, and my second wife's love for me wasn't as strong as mine was for her. For some reason things don't always turn out the way you plan, no matter how well they are thought out.

I still remember the day my one and only daughter was born. The delivery day started at home when Patsy, my wife, looked at me and said it was time to go to the hospital. I got her there on time, and as I stood next to her, holding her hand, I watched the machine that she was hooked up to. It consisted of a pen writing on graft paper, and it kept going up and down charting the birth pains as they got stronger. I didn't need the graft though, to tell me the pain was increasing, because her hand squeezing mine was letting me know. I felt so helpless watching the needle slowly increase until it reached a point, and then just fall away to the bottom of the graft, signifying the pain had stopped until the next contraction.

The doctor came in and said, "Let me take a look." Then he told me I'd better get dressed in a hospital robe if I wanted to help in the operating room. I had no idea that I was going to come and watch our daughter being born, let alone help. We had not planned that at all, but Patsy's hand in mine, and the look in her eyes, told me that was what I was going to do.

So off I went to the operating room to witness the miracle of birth and give a helping hand. I remember standing there feeling quite stupid and useless, and hearing the doctor give instructions: "Now when I say push, you push." Then in a little while I heard "push" a couple of times, then, "its coming," and then, "there's the head," then finally "it's a girl" Then I heard a small cry. Our daughter was born and the blood in my hand started to come back as Pasty stopped squeezing it.

After my wife had given birth, they all hurried away to put the baby in an incubator to help remove a slight sign of jaundice. Patsy lay alone in the operating room on a metal table. It was like they had all forgotten the mother and left her to fend for herself. All eyes seemed to be on the baby, including mine.

We were in the hospital on Patuxent Navy Air Base in Maryland. We were the only couple in the maternity ward, and April, later to be named, was the only baby in the ward. The drive home by myself later that night was one of the loneliest times I can remember in my life. I just didn't want to leave my wife and new daughter.

Flowers the next day were in order, and I just didn't know how to act. I was the proud father of a beautiful baby girl, and I had helped deliver her into the world. We named her April Ann, and she gets more beautiful each year.

Hollywood Elem.
Hollywood Md
April 29, 1988

Dear Dad,
    Hi, I wanted to tell you some things I've never told you before. THANK YOU! THANK YOU! for being a wounderful DAD, and THANK YOU! for buying my bunk bed, and THANK YOU! for being just the way you are, and THANK YOU! for standing up for yourself and THANK YOU! for believing in god, and THANK YOU! for reading this letter.

                Love,
                April

P.S. and Thank You! For being my father

128

<u>89th Military Airlift Wing</u>

I represented the 89th Military Airlift Wing located at Andrews Air Force Base, Maryland, and there I was designated by the White House and the United States Air Force to represent the United States of America. For ten years I was a flight steward or, as we referred to it in the galley, an airborne zoological dietician and mixologist. In layman's terms, we fed the animals while at the airborne watering hole. I was like a mother robin feeding her young. As I used to walk up and down the aisles of our VC135 aircraft, which was configured with plush seating, dining tables, and bunking compartments, and while traveling to many worldwide destinations, I made myself available for whatever our distinguished passengers might

129

want. I tried to always look with expectancy and a smile, and to present a pleasing manner to accommodate my passengers' every need. As baby chicks in a nest open their mouths for food, I saw mouths opening and demanding from me whatever service we could provide.

I offered coffee, tea, and whatever else was requested or required. It all started after my first divorce out in California from Gayle, a little North Carolina girl who was not happy with me and who started searching for new areas of romance after seven years of marriage. I worked in ground traffic control at Travis Air Force Base at the time, when a recruiting scout came into my office looking for volunteers for flight stewards to work in the presidential squadron. Not only did I want to get away from Gayle and a bad marriage, but traveling first class around the world sounded ok to me.

It took one year for me to get a top secret clearance though, because they physically had to check out every item on my personal history application, and I had moved around a lot during my life, sometimes twice a year. When the Federal Bureau of Investigations sent agents around to check out my information, some people were afraid to say they knew me. Others could not be found and I had to resubmit for that time period. But patience and persistence did have their reward, and eventually I was granted a top secret clearance. I finally received orders for my new assignment after a year of waiting, wondering, and submitting paperwork.

I took leave and visited Mom and Dad in Idaho, and we celebrated the good news of my new job along with the bad news of my divorce. I then reported to my new duty station, not knowing what to expect, but glad to be starting over. I was single, with a new apartment, a new job, new furniture, a new car, and starting a new life.

The first thing I had to do was get on flying status which meant getting a passport, updating my shots, being altitude chamber tested, passing a physical, and being issued new clothing, most of which I had taken care of at Travis Air Force Base before coming to Andrews Air Force Base. After finishing all that, I was officially assigned to the 98th Military Airlift Squadron which meant I would be flying the heavies: VC137s and VC135s, which are like Boeing 707 aircraft made for long range, worldwide transportation.

My first trip was to Honolulu, Hawaii. We carried 5 passengers and stayed at a hotel on the beach for a week, then returned our passengers to Andrews. Staying with the passengers was necessary in case they needed anything, or in case they had to contact us quickly or leave the area.

The amazing thing was our time was our own while we were on the ground. We did shop for some pineapples and other fruits for the aircraft, but it was just like a paid Hawaiian vacation. While we were there, I learned how to make a pineapple boat as a salad, and after that I served it many times when I traveled around the world. All the meals I served on board the aircraft were made from scratch. I learned how to prepare Mahi-Mahi covered with sautéed almonds in a sweet lemon butter sauce. If I didn't know how to present or cook something, I went out before the trip and ordered it at the best restaurant I could find, and then served it that way on the aircraft. I ate Peking Duck in the Peking Restaurant, in Peking, China, mainly because I wanted to know how to serve it if asked to do so. I did the same with drinks because I provided a full bar aboard, including wines with the meals. Having tasted wine in a dark amber bottle from the Rhine River area in Germany, and wine in a green bottle from the Morsel River area, I knew the difference. We used real china and silverware on board, and the silverware had to be dipped after breakfast because eggs tarnished the silver. We also washed our own dishes, providing better security for our passengers.

Before leaving on a trip, I always made recommendations and coordinated with the person in charge of the traveling party, who I presented the fare to. He or she acted as a liaison between the passengers and I, which represented the aircraft commander of the 98th Military Airlift Squadron.

The White House authorizes these trips for their distinguished guests, who could be Presidents, Kings or Queens, Generals, Senators, Congressmen, and/or Statesmen from all over the world. The White House sent their requirements to the 89th Military Airlift Wing and we carried out their orders, putting America's best foot forward.

I retired from the United States Air Force and my position with the 89th Military Airlift Wing in September of 1981, but its memories I will always carry with me. When I think of America, I will always think of the best, for I know I gave it mine.

Gary Fowler
gets pay bonus

CAMP SPRINGS, Md.— Staff Sergeant Gary H. Fowler, son of Mr. and Mrs. W. A. Reineke of Sandpoint, has been named one of the top 15 per cent in his Air Force specialty. He will receive a superior performance pay bonus for six months as a result of his selection.

The sergeant, a flight traffic specialist, was chosen for his leadership, exemplary conduct, technical skill and duty performance in competition with all other airmen in his grade and specialty.

He is presently serving at Andrews AFB, Md., with the 89th Military Airlift Wing, the special Air Force unit which provides air transportation for the President of the United States and other top government officials.

Sergeant Fowler, who has served in Vietnam, attended Milligan High School, Long Beach, Calif. He completed the requirements for his diploma after entering the service. The sergeant has attended the University of Maryland Far East Division, Japan, the University of Guam and the University of Salano, Fairfield, Calif.

133

Cooking

The 89th Military Airlift Wing provided the opportunity for me to go to a culinary arts school at Fort Lee Army Camp in Virginia. There they instruct chefs from all over the military in the art of meat cutting, ice carving, and how to provide meals of all kinds for large groups. I went there to learn how to make different sauces.

While I was there, I learned to carve a dolphin out of a 250 pound block of ice. I used the dolphin carving to chill some cooked shrimp, along with a homemade cocktail sauce that I learned to make. The dolphin stood on its head with the shrimp in its lower lip and the cocktail sauce in its smaller upper lip. This shrimp and cocktail sauce was part of a finger food buffet held at the Fort Lee Officer's Club. There, for training purposes, we made finger sandwiches, hors d'oeuvres, and other culinary delights all garnished for eye appeal.

The 89th MAW also sent folks to another school, located in New York City, New York. What they taught there was how to run and manage an Officer or NCO Club, and how to manage a night club and restaurant for a military base. This was a civilian school where major hotel chains sent their managers for training. Not many of us got to attend this school, mainly because of the time it took to complete, which was about three months.

I learned most of my cooking skills on the aircraft by watching other flight attendants. But sometimes I would go out to a fine restaurant just to see how a particular dish was prepared. Our cooking facilities on board the aircraft were a lot different than those in a standard kitchen. The environment consisted of a pressurized cabin, air changing every six minutes, turbulence at unexpected times, and very close quarters. Our cooking equipment included four whirlwind ovens, dry ice for refrigeration, and limited storage space. Additionally, we had to maintain a bar and beverage counter for our passengers and cater to their immediate requests, providing snacks cigarettes, matches, mints, and special items like jellybeans for President Reagan.

Sometimes we would carry over 100 passengers and we had to provide a full meal for them in little over an hour, including take off and landing. This required a great deal of planning. For example, if we had to make steak dinners for over 100 in less than an hour's flight time, we had the steaks cooked rare at the NCO club prior to the flight so we could finish them to order onboard. The steaks still had the grilled design of the grate on them even though we would finish cooking them on a flat grill on board the aircraft.

We baked potatoes in our whirlwind ovens on the ground, and our vegetables we cooked in the fourth oven which was on the plane. Before takeoff, we set up our tray carriers with tossed salads,

135

silverware, napkins, and mints. We had to double them up because we had only two tray carriers, and each held only 24 trays. Doubling them gave us 96 placements. The trays had to be stacked on each other. The remaining four placements were usually set up separately at the Distinguished Visitor's Table. The desert was usually cake or cheesecake, which we had cut and placed on a dish in the freezer beforehand. After takeoff we took drink and steak orders from the passengers, served them dinner and drinks within 20 minutes into the flight, and refreshed their drinks during the next 30 minutes. Next we collected all the trays and dishes from the distinguished visitor's table and loaded them back into the tray carriers before landing. Usually we finished cleaning up after the passengers were off the aircraft, but sometimes, if everything went well and I had a good crew, we finished most of the cleaning before landing.

Most of the time however, our aircraft was set up with only five tables and carried less than 20 passengers, for whom we provided full dining room services. This was aboard the VC 135 aircraft. The VC 137 was configured with different equipment, but the game plan was the same.

We bought all our food and supplies commercially, providing only the best for our passengers. We always tried to give the best service we could as well. This is how we got our nickname of "SAM fox." SAM stood for Special Airlift Missions, and the fox denoted wisdom, as in "crafty as a fox."

To The Men & Marines of the 89th M.A.W.

United States Senate Restaurant

Senator Hartke and his lovely wife Martha invited us to dinner at the United States Senate Restaurant in the Capital Building on returning from Spain in 1973, because of our service aboard the 89th MAW mission.

Arabian Knights

We were staying in the same hotel that President Theodore Roosevelt loved to stay at, and where he conducted some of his fireside chats when he went to Cairo, Egypt. Waking up and opening the curtains in my hotel room, I couldn't believe the view from the window. What I saw were the three Great Pyramids, close enough that I thought I could have thrown a rock from my window and hit them.

It was my first time to Cairo and we had gotten to the hotel after 12:00 a.m. from the aircraft. Taking care of the passengers first, we then wanted to clean and refuel the plane and have it ready for our next leg to Tel Aviv, Israel, before we left for the hotel. We didn't get a chance to see much of the surrounding area since there wasn't much outside, nor was there street lighting that early in the morning when we checked in.

The hotel was first class and even had its own horse stables. After breakfast some of the crew members and I rented horses and hired a guide to ride out into the desert and visit some of the nearby tombs. By the time we got back my legs were so sore that I couldn't lift them to get off my horse. The guide had to raise one of my legs to swing it over the horse so I could get off. He invited us into his house for something to eat, and we accepted, not wanting to be rude.

He lived with his wife and three children in an adobe hut with a dirt floor. It had a small uncovered courtyard and one room for living quarters. His wife wasn't there but he offered us some dates and banana pieces and we each took one. He was very polite and asked if we wanted to ride out that night to an Arab coffee house and see a belly dancer. The guys said yes, and I told him I would have to let him know because I didn't know how my legs would feel. That night my legs were better so I went with the other crew members.

We rode out over the desert sands in the moonlight, like some Arabian knights, to a tent in the middle of nowhere. We sat on the floor on carpets, drank coffee, tea, and ate rice cakes, while watching a belly dancer do her thing. It was like being in some kind of Casablanca movie; I kept waiting for Humphrey Bogart to say "Play it again Sam." Riding back to the hotel it was cold but the heat from my horse kept me warm. My Pentex Spotmactic camera beat against my side as I held on to this white Arabian stallion I had rented, while we galloped across the sand dunes to the hotel. I was surprised that I didn't have trouble getting off the horse this time.

139

We had two and a half days on the ground at Cairo and the second day I walked out to the Great Pyramid and went up inside of it. The huge stones were placed so close together you couldn't get a piece of paper between them, and the tour guide said they weighed over six thousand pounds with some weighing as much as ten thousand pounds. The smoke from the torches that the slaves carried to light the way into the upper chamber, where the king was buried, were still on the ceiling and walls. These slaves were buried alive along with their dead king. Writings were still legible on the walls if you could read Egyptian. But most of what we saw were ruins waiting for time to finish the job.

That night a couple of crew members and I went to see the laser light show at the foot of The Great Pyramids. They had seats set up in front of the Sphinx, and laser lights would point out historical points of different areas as they told us how mighty generals, like Alexander the Great had come and fought and tried to conquer the land. Alexander the Great was the one who blew off the nose of the Sphinx with a cannon. But the narrator explained that Egypt still remains today, after all those mighty generals were dead and gone.

I never did ride a camel, but that pure Arabian stallion I rode through the desert that one night, and the real belly dancer, I will never forget.

Russia

It was like walking into a history book as I went through Red Square in Moscow. Lenin's tomb was to my right, kids dressed like boy and girl scouts marched in single file toward the spot in some kind of precision formation, and Russian guards were in the area, spit and polished. To my left were the Russian Orthodox Catholic Churches. Their turban top roofs were painted bright carnival colors and trimmed in gold for all to see, now used only for museums for tourism. High walls with towers at each corner ran along the river near the square.

Russia and the United States had gone into space

together and the U. S. S. R. government had now invited the
American astronauts to their country. I was the steward in charge of
the flight for the 89th Military Airlift Wing, providing in-flight
accommodations for both countries' astronauts, and I got a first class
tour of Moscow. The tour began at the Bolshoi Ballet where we

had front
row seats
right behind
the orchestra
and in the
middle of the
opera hall.
Talking
about stereo,
I never

enjoyed anything as much as The Nutcracker Suite with the
performing Russia troupe players. You could hear every note from
each instrument in the orchestra and see each player so gracefully
performing each movement. The embassy had made the arrangements
and the Russian government provided the seats. I was a happy
camper.

You would think that would have been enough for anyone
for one day, but that evening we were taken to a tower that had a
revolving restaurant overlooking the city of Moscow. The prime
purpose for the tower was radio transmission, and at the very top was
radio transmitting equipment. I was told that the restaurant, which

was just below, was for entertaining government guests and elite personnel of the government. Lucky me. Right time, right place.

The food was pretty good, but they cut their meat differently than we do, making it kind of tough to chew. I had the steak, and like I said, it was ok. The best part came as we ate our desert—delicious chocolate mousse. The restaurant revolved, and at about dawn we were overlooking the city of Moscow. Fireworks erupted over the whole city, outlining an already beautiful skyline, with the picturesque city of Moscow in full view. Unfortunately, I forgot my camera. I realized that our two governments did have something in common, and I had a trip to remember.

I have been back to Russia since then, and another best was their circus. I have seen a lot of circuses but nothing as good as what I saw in Mother Russia, which was the theme of their circus. At the end of the show, a girl carried a loaf of bread into the center ring, simulating Mother Russia feeding the people. Just like I said before, some good, some bad. Some philosophies you have to chew on, others are universal.

People I Met

Some of the people I have met have made history, not only during their own lives, but during mine.

There was Ronald Reagan who started out as a movie star; I still remember watching his movies. Then he ran for California Governor and took California from the red into the black financially. I remember him saying he would save California money by not buying new envelopes for his office. He instructed his staff to cross out the old Governor's name and type his in. He said there was a certain satisfaction in doing that. I can't even remember the old Governor's name now. I flew with him, when he was Governor Reagan, to Hawaii, Australia, China, and back, and I still would give him my vote; just as I did when he ran for President of the United States and won. It was his letter of commendation that helped land me a new job when I got out of the United States Air Force and stopped flying with the 98th Military Airlift Squadron. I felt the sorrow of the whole nation as his funeral was shown on television, and I felt so sad for his beloved wife Nancy, who I also had the pleasure of meeting.

Vice President Walter F. Mondale also sent me a letter of commendation. We flew together many times during his administration and he was pleased with the excellent support given him. I also had the honor of being reenlisted by this Vice President.

Another person that I had the honor of being reenlisted by was President Bush senior. He was Vice President at the time, but that didn't lessen the honor for me. During a reenlistment ceremony, the American flag is supposed to be in the background, but we didn't have one inside the aircraft, so I was told that they used the flag that was painted on the tail of the aircraft as the reenlistment flag. We were about 35,000 feet in the air and on our way to Europe at the time, if I remember right. The suit I am wearing in this picture is my duty uniform which I wore when traveling as a 98th Military Airlift Squadron flight attendant. The different countries we went to did not like having United States military uniforms parading around, so we wore business suits while performing our duties. The rest of the crew also wore suits, depending on what country we were flying into.

I guess The President I liked the most was Gerald Ford. I flew with him on his 25th wedding anniversary, and I remember the press giving him 25 silver quarters pasted on a card representing the 25 years of wedded bliss. I carved a turkey out of an apple for his table on that trip. I put it on a bed of lettuce/parsley with butter patties around it, and made it a centerpiece as well as a butter dish for the table.

Presidents and Vice Presidents weren't the only people I met during my travels with the 89th. I can remember Senator Henry M. Jackson, Senator Robert P. Griffin, Senator Frank E. Moss, and the Minority Floor Leader, Senator J. Glenn Beall, Jr. of Maryland; I also met Senator Hartke and his lovely wife Martha. They invited us to the United States Senate Restaurant where I had a bowl of that famous Senate Restaurant bean soup, which cost 45 cents back then, but the fare was on the Senator and his wife.

And of course I can't leave out the House of Representatives. I recall Bob Casey of Texas, Goodloe E. Byron of the 6th District in Maryland, Claude Pepper of the 14th District in Florida, and many more. I also provided logistical support for the Postmaster General, William F. Bolger and his delegation to China and Japan, and the Under Secretary of the Treasury, Paul A. Volcker during a trip to Tokyo. I met the Honorable Frederick Dent, the Secretary of Commerce, one year during a trip to Buenos Aires. It was the 4th of July and I remember that we landed in heavy fog, making several passes over the air field at night before we finally could see to land. On the way home, I produced a July 4th birthday cake bedecked with flags and sparklers.

I am extremely proud of the letter of appreciation I received from Mr. Warren Christopher, Department of State, for the part we played in the release and subsequent return to American control of the 52 Americans held hostage in Iran. I remember it was raining when we arrived in Algiers for the final round of negotiations, and I escorted Mr. Christopher with an umbrella from the aircraft to the air terminal. The television camera lights were blinding us as we walked and he said, "Stay close to me." Later when I returned home, my wife Patsy said she saw us on television that night. I must have stayed close to the man.

The Lord has blessed me, and may He continue to bless not only me, but America. Amen.

A Touch From Behind

To M/Sgt. Gary Fowler - With
Thanks For Everything + Best Regards
Nancy + Ronald Reagan

We had just arrived at Anderson Air Force Base, Guam and had begun refueling for our onward trip to Sidney, Australia. It was late evening there, but the moon was out and the weather was tropical, with a gentle wind blowing across the island. I had been flying as a flight steward in the 89th Military Airlift Wing for a couple of years and was looking forward to this trip.

Governor Ronald Reagan had gotten up from his bed aboard the 98th Military Airlift Squardron's VC135, and walked into the air terminal to look around, waiting for the plane to be refueled. His wife, Mrs. Nancy Reagan, was still in her bunk, which was up over his bunk aboard the aircraft. The lights in the aircraft were off because we didn't have a waiver from the Department of Defense to run the power generator and refuel the aircraft at the same time. The only other lights aboard the aircraft

148

were flashlights which the engineer and flight stewards carried; and they were busy trying to get the aircraft ready for the next leg of the trip, checking all the safety gear, servicing the toilets, removing the trash, replacing the used potable water aboard. Most of the other passengers, about ten, stayed aboard in their seats and continued their naps. It had been a long trip from Honolulu, Hawaii to Guam, and it was going to be an even longer trip to Sidney, Australia. However, a few passengers, about three, did go into the air terminal with Governor Reagan.

Four other stewards and I were busy straightening up the aircraft and trying to think of anything else we needed before continuing on. Unlike our counterparts in civilian life, we planned and prepared all the meals from scratch while maintaining a full bar with such things as cigarettes, cigars, candy, chips, pretzels, nuts, and any special items like the jelly beans Governor Reagan liked. We kept a bowl of jelly beans on his table the whole trip; not that he asked for them, but we got to know our passengers very well in order to service their needs and make them feel at home. Traveling from Honolulu, Hawaii to Sidney, Australia, then to both Singapore and Peking, China, then on to Yokota Air Base, Japan, and back to Andrews Air Force Base, Maryland was about a three week trip, and it was our job to put the White House's best foot forward. We also handled the baggage and any other personal items for the passengers. We were like their butlers in the sky, and first class was the name of the game. Anything our passengers wanted we provided. Our meals were as good as those of any first class restaurant, and the service was as good as that of any five star hotel. This called for a lot of preplanning because there are no Seven-Eleven stores at 40,000 feet, but it was our job and we were good at it. For safety reasons, we bought most of our supplies before leaving Andrews Air Force Base. Produce and meats were best purchased in the United States, and because we had no power on the aircraft at our overseas destinations, we refrigerated all perishable items with dry ice.

I had just finished servicing the coffee area in the front of the plane and started back to the galley, which was located in the tail of the aircraft, to check on our dry ice supply. When I got to the stateroom sleeping quarters, Mrs. Reagan opened her draw curtain and asked me what we were doing. I told her we had arrived in Guam and that her husband had gone into the air terminal until we were ready to depart. I explained that the aircraft was being refueled, which was the reason the lights were out. I offered to give her a hand down from her bed, and she started to get out of the top bunk. The carpet was made of nylon fiber and the air in the aircraft was very dry because of the high altitude flight we had just taken, and when I reached up to help her down, a spark from my index finger landed on her posterior with a loud zapping noise. She has big beautiful eyes to begin with, but at that moment, they seemed extra large and trained on me. I could feel myself blushing and was at a loss for words. She didn't say anything, she only smiled and got out of the bunk by herself. I still can remember the zapping noise, a small ouch sound, and some very fast movement in the top bunk that night. All that from "a touch from behind," or a memoir from the past.

This Little Old Jug Of Mine

In my living room sits a juglet that was dated by an archeologist back to 800 B.C. Not only is it old, but the expert I got it from said it was found near the Wailing Wall in Jerusalem, Israel. I bought it in Tel Aviv, Israel while walking along the Mediterranean Sea.

I noticed a small shop with artifacts in the window, so I went in to look around. I wanted a souvenir from Israel, and there was a little black juglet, about two inches high and one inch wide. It had a handle on its side, making it look like a water pitcher. It also had a small jagged piece missing from it. At the time, though I knew it was old, I didn't really know how old, but I did think it was reasonable for it to have some damage.

I bargained with the shopkeeper for a price I could afford, and as I was ready to walk out the door with my prize, he told me he would get me one that was not broken. I started to wonder if he was making these juglets in the back room. He pulled out a wooden box, and there must have been ten of the same juglets in there, three of which were not broken. He handed me one of the unbroken ones. He then   introduced himself as the archeologist that was present when these artifacts were uncovered. He showed me his credentials, then took out a certificate and hand drew the juglet onto it, placed the national seal on it, and signed it. He asked me if I would like a bag to carry it in. Just like Wal Mart, I thought.

Still kind of in shock from seeing the other nine juglets, I looked at the certificate to see just how old this thing was. I read that it was dated between 600 to 800 B.C. He then said that it was found near the Wailing Wall, but that he couldn't put that on the certificate which read "excavated near Jerusalem."

I thanked him and left the store, still wondering just what was true, if anything, about this little juglet of mine.

Aircraft Carriers

I have traveled the seven seas on most of the United States Naval Aircraft Carriers and the flight deck is the most dangerous place I have ever been. Yes, I have even

seen people killed during my travels on the decks of these enormous vessels. Yet, these ships protect and defend our nation and are our best deterrent against world aggression.

One particular time, I had just finished two weeks of work onboard one aircraft carrier. I was about to be loaded on a cod— a two engine, propeller driven transport aircraft— and returned to the beach for transportation home to Patuxent Naval Air Station.

I lost that ride however, because of a cracked propeller caused by a very tragic accident.

There was a young sailor whose job it was to handle and support these carrier aircraft. He had forgotten where the propellers were located on our cod, which was doing a pre-flight departure run up, and as he backed up to get out of the way of an F-14 fighter jet's exhaust, he backed into a revolving prop on the left side of our aircraft. The F-14 pilot had been turning onto the catapult and never saw the young sailor. Eight plastic bags were used to gather his remains. He hadn't been married long, and that day his young pregnant wife lost her husband; his unborn child lost his or her father; the Navy lost a good sailor; America lost a patriotic citizen; and many sailors lost a good shipmate. I remember seeing a sailor who probably weighed about 260 pounds and stood about 6 feet 7 seven inches tall, coming down the stairwell from the flight deck after the accident. Both his hands were bloody, and he was holding his head and crying because he had taken a flying dive onto the flight deck, trying and failing to reach and save his shipboard buddy's life. All this happened because of a little poor judgment on the part of a young sailor who was away from home serving his country. We all lost that day. I believe the pilot of that F-14 will always wonder if he was at fault.

Another time on another carrier I witnessed another tragedy. Two fire fighters were hosing down the fight deck to remove a gas spill when their stream of water went into an electrical outlet that had been left open. As I was setting up a camera on the 08 level, which is on the island of the flight deck, I saw the fireman holding the hose being electrocuted, then being rushed to the medical station onboard. Those were men just doing their jobs, protecting our nation, and they were injured on duty through no mistake on their part. When small mistakes are made, accidents happen and can be deadly on a flight deck.

The jet blast of a fighter plane can produce 200 mile an hour winds at idle speed, and can blow a man off the ship in the blink of an eye. The jet engine's intake can also pull a full grown man off his feet and into the engine in a matter of seconds. Aircraft carrier decks are no place to be daydreaming.

For over 15 years it was a part of my job to test equipment and photograph aircraft from an aircraft carrier's deck. I used to stand between the catapults on the flight deck, providing film and video coverage of aircraft taking off. Those were called "cat shots." Then I'd walk over to the landing side of the flight deck and photograph the aircraft landings, called "traps," as they caught on one of four wires spread across the flight deck.

The vibrations and noise were louder than any rock concert, even if you were standing in front of the speakers. And like the mistakes that I mentioned before, when and if they happened it was "Katie bar the door"; there was no makeup point. You had to be aware of your environment at all times, and even then you were not assured of a safe return home. But the job was exciting and rewarding for this traveling photographer.

I remember the steel beach parties, where the captain of the ship would anchor off shore, and break out the bar-b-que grills, steaks, burgers, hot dogs, baked beans, potato salad, and sodas. The captain would then let down the elevators, which were used to raise the aircraft from the hanger bay to the flight deck, so the crew could go fishing. There we'd sit on the edge of the elevator, eating burgers and drinking sodas with fishing poles in our hands, looking for the big one. The captain would also have the communication section tune in on the latest football games by satellite, then pipe them throughout the ship. The ships also had their own local rock groups, which was ship's company, on the fight deck playing their favorite songs with electric guitars, keyboards, drums and the group's best singer. If you were into a healthier lifestyle, you could always jog around the flight deck or lift weights from a bench-press set up on the flight deck. That's what a steel beach party was like.

Shock trials, were also exciting and kind of like being in a James Bond movie, with 50,000 lbs. of explosives being detonated in the water only 500 feet from you. Believe me, that will get you off your feet, get your heart going, and keep your attention as you watch debris fall from the ceiling and the walls fall out around you. It definitely gives you something to write home about.

Cat shots and traps, or landings, are always fun to watch. I had been shot off of an aircraft carrier many times from the catapult and landed or trapped by a wire on the flight deck more times than I can remember, but the thrill is always there. I guess it's the unknown that keeps your attention, not knowing when we were going to go on the cat shots, and if we were going to stop on the traps.

From the flight deck of an aircraft carrier to the water is around 90 feet straight down, quite a high dive for even the best of divers. I was on a carrier during a hurricane, and I saw waves breaking 30 feet over the flight deck that tore a twenty man lift raft off

156

the front of this huge ship, damaging the catwalks up forward. I also saw marines with their noses up against the portholes in the front of the ship, waiting for the next wave to hit. The glass never broke.

I have seen aircraft pilots forget to release their brakes on takeoff while on the catapult, blowing out all their tires because the flight deck is covered with nonskid. The nonskid is so rough that it will wear out a pair of shoes in a couple of weeks. Those aircraft with blown tires could not return and land aboard the carrier. They had to return to the beach and land on a foam covered runway. This is another mistake any one of us could have made that resulted in the pilot having an emergency on his hands.

Life onboard was not all excitement though. I remember seeing aircraft carriers dump their trash at sea in plastic bags, leaving a trail of these bags as far as the eye can see behind the ship. And I recall thinking that there must be a better way. That was the only time I can remember not being proud of the ship I was on.

Carrier life is like no other, with all its smells and noises. There is the smell of steam and the noise of the shuttle, which the aircraft is connected to on the catapult, as it hits the break at the end of its run. I can remember being awakened by this sound, which is much like dropping a piece of iron from a hundred feet up onto another piece of iron on the ground. I rose up out of bed so fast I hit my head on the bunk over me, not knowing what had happened. These were just morning checks for the ship.

Standing in the hanger bay, I remember seeing flying fish trying to get out of the way of the ship and gliding 50 to 60 feet in the air over the waves. I also saw porpoises swimming in front of the ship, listening to the sonar that seemed to be calling to them. The ships even have their own vocabulary, "Gee dunk" means a place to buy candy and snacks; "head" is a bathroom; "sand crabs" are civilians; and the "XO" is the executive officer in charge of the ship.

There is something special about the call of the sea which I am at a loss to explain. Maybe it's the breeze and the salt air hitting your face or perhaps the waves on top of the water that call to you. Perhaps it's the smell of salt air and sea foam penetrating your nostrils, or the thought of what's out there and where it may lead. I can't explain it, but there is a call nonetheless.

I have crossed the equator, and I have met King Neptune in a ceremony that has been held from the beginning of time by all sailors. These ships are powered by nuclear engines instead of sails, but the trip is the same; only the times are different.

There are a lot of other things I recall from my trips with these aircraft carriers as well. I remember how the water swirls down the toilet bowl but goes in the opposite direction after you cross the equator. I remember different types of carriers, like the USS Lexington, which had a wooden deck; I remember which had the best food, like the USS Enterprise; which treated you the best, like the USS Midway, and which one had the best accommodations, like the USS Roosevelt.

But as the people changed, so did the ships and all have their good and bad points at one time or another. I guess it was really the people, not the ships, I remember the most.

In 1998 I stopped working aboard these floating cities
that travel the world carrying five to six thousand men and women. I
now track and photograph these same aircraft from the beach, with
large telescopes and high speed cameras.

Tell Two

This was not the Chinese restaurant we wanted to eat at.

Show Two

We wanted to try the food in a new Chinese restaurant in Golden Beach, Maryland. We went in and sat down, and soon the waitress brought us a menu and a pot of hot tea. She said that she would be right back to take our orders. I like hot tea, so I picked up the pot and poured some into a small cup that was in front of me. When I had finished, a cockroach was swimming in the middle of my cup. This was not the restaurant we wanted to eat at. We got up and walked out, leaving the tea for the bugs.

Patuxent Baptist Church

Patuxent Baptist Church in Hollywood, Maryland had a very interesting beginning. It started out as a tin building, located on Route 235 and Mervell Dean Road. When it was discovered that the contractors never applied for a building permit, but told the zoning commission it was only a warehouse, and then marked it as office space, it should have been the end. Fortunately, some political maneuvering allowed the building to remain standing.

At first, it was a warehouse. Next, it became an office building to sell swimming pools. Then it provided office space for the Republican Central Committee Headquarters. Eventually it housed an African American beauty salon, as well as office space for insurance agents to conduct business. Finally, it became Patuxent Baptist Church, headed by an Independent Baptist man who was called of God to preach salvation by grace.

Pastor Rick Conner received his salvation by grace listening to the radio and then received his calling at Independent Baptist Church in Clinton, Maryland. After that, he attended Hyles

Anderson Independent Baptist College in Indiana, and was led of God to bring the gospel to Hollywood, Maryland.

I first knew of Pastor Conner from an ad I read in the Enterprise newspaper. The ad said, "God doesn't like long hair." Being divorced and trying to raise a daughter, I needed God's help, and this seemed to me to be the answer—a bible believing church right in Hollywood. So I visited one Sunday morning. From that point on, I felt God wanted me to support this small church with whatever I had.

The first thing I did for the church was make a three dimensional wooden cross for the front of their sanctuary. Next, I made a stained glass window which said, "Jesus Saves" with a cross and a dove in the background. The church needed a flag stand for two flags, the American flag and the Christian flag, which the ladies of the church had bought. I made the flag stands from oak and walnut wood which came from my backyard, and I cured the wood over a stove in my garage. Next, I made another stained glass window, with praying hands and a cross in the background, because the church had only two windows in its auditorium.

The church began to grow, and for the families that attended, I made many miniature wooden crosses from the same kind of wood as the first large cross in the sanctuary: mahogany, black walnut, and dogwood. Dogwood is a white wood, and to me it represented purity; black walnut is a darker wood, representing man's sin; and mahogany is a reddish wood, which I felt represented the blood of Christ, which everything hangs on. I placed the black walnut between the dogwood and mahogany, three crosses on top of one another. I believe the

162

design came from God; without the mahogany, or blood of Christ, man could never see God.

I gave these crosses to every family in the church in an effort to help increase the congregation. I also made many stained glass signs and items for the church and congregation; and I presented them to our pastor and missionaries whenever the opportunity presented itself.

As I tried to help increase our congregation and the calling of Christ, I saw many people come and go. I also tried to keep a pictorial record of the talented souls who gave their all for the gospel. Some of them later fell away, while others stayed their course and furthered the kingdom of our Lord.

The Spirit has always been strong in this church. With thanksgiving, love, and service, we reach out to one another in Christian love and worship Jesus in love and truth. I look forward to the near approaching rapture, which is foretold in the bible. Jesus has always given me His best, and I am thankful to have been given the opportunity to serve Him in this church with the talents and gifts He has provided me. So until His return, I say preach on Pastor!

This is our new church building.

The Tracker

Gary is my name and tracking is my game—or for the past 25 years it has been. I now work for Computer Science Corporation (CSC), who took over DynCorp, my old boss, who had bought Dyn-a-Electron, my first employer, after I retired from the military. Like fish in the ocean, the bigger ones keep swallowing the little ones, companies that is. But knowledge and experience are what these companies feed on, and fortunately I have both in the technical fields of photography and computer science, combined with world wide travel knowledge. I'm 64 years old and employed at a Navy tracking station where I provide digital pictures and digital video with longitude, latitude, and distance, denoting (XYZ) computer data, combined with real time measuring increments. Engineers use this information to set certain perimeters on our weapon systems and study them to improve our military equipment and its readiness, testing each of their different criteria.

I use a kinetic tracking mount with a large telescopic lens, connected to high speed video and infrared cameras. These cameras are able to see and record things within inches, things which are miles away in space and traveling at high speeds, even through haze. They bring them into view to be studied and recorded for future study, or to provide instant replay of any weapon system being tracked, stopping the movement for on-the-spot evaluation. To me it's like playing a video game and seeing how close I can keep the crosshair on the target I am tracking. 25 years of experience has made me a very good tracker and I enjoy what I do very much. The equipment I use gets more technical and the working facilities improve every year, but the job remains the same.

Some of our video has been used commercially, like the crash scene in the movie "Top Gun," which really happened. It was photographed from Bay Forest Tracking Station here in St. Mary's County. The real pilots ejected out of the F-14 fighter which crashed into the Chesapeake Bay, and we tracked them all the way to impact.

"Hi angle of attack" refers to when a plane goes to 40,000 feet or better and stalls out its engines, letting the aircraft free fall back to earth while we record what happens during the free fall. This information tells pilots what to expect of their aircraft if this should happen under uncontrolled circumstances and how to recover from a stalled engine. I track and record all this information giving them real time, weather conditions, and a video recording of exactly what happened. This also tells them just how much force the aircraft can withstand and what improvements to make.

Additionally, I record and monitor different weapon systems being deployed from these aircraft. I record how they react and what effect they have on the aircraft carrying them. We track weather balloons, measuring speed and wind direction so we know just how much the weather affects our systems. We use mathematics in everything we do because they need to know, down to the inch, just what happened, which is why close tracking is so important.

I am very proud of my tracking record, so I feel sorry each time I miss or can't see a target and end up giving them no data. I'm glad to say that doesn't happen often. I guess that's what makes me a good tracker.

This is a A6 aircraft.

Shock Trials

I was waiting for 50,000 lbs. of explosives to go off 500 feet from me. I had made everything ready; my cameras were in place and loaded with high speed film and set for 400 frames per second. The Navy had given me the job of capturing a photographic record of the shock trial for the Aircraft Carrier USS Theodore Roosevelt CVN-71. They needed to see what effect a bomb would have if dropped that close to one of their ships. I wasn't the only photographer there; others had also set up cameras on different parts of the ship. I was waiting for them to set the explosive off which was located 500 feet from the right side of the Aircraft Carrier and 50 feet down in the water. A spotter had circled in a helicopter looking for any fish in the area, and had given his all clear signal. This area was chosen because of the lack of sea life, but a routine check was always a wise move. The count down began over the ship's intercom speakers: "Event in minus 10, 9, 8, 7, 6, 5," and I turned on my cameras at the count of 5 by remote switch.

I had designed special camera mounts for these shock trials so that the initial blast would not move the cameras before photographs could be taken at 400 frames per second, showing every little movement in the area at the initial time of the blast. I did this with bungee cords in a metal frame. The frame would move with the initial shock, but the weight of the camera on the elastic bungee cords prevented movement of the cameras until after photographing the movement of the initial shock on the affected area. In short, I got what I wanted in pictures, and timing was put on the film by the camera's matrix.

The blast itself lifted me off the floor about a foot. Things that had been left in the ceiling of the hanger bay by maintenance men, like welding rods, pop cans, nails, lost tools, etc., fell from the 40 foot high ceiling to the hanger bay floor. I had one camera in the hanger bay and two on the flight deck, which by now was covered with water. The blast's wake covered the ship with tons of water spray, so it was a good thing I had used plastic bags to cover my flight deck cameras.

One of the cameras on the flight deck was focused on an A7 aircraft which seemed to survive the shock very well. The other one, however, was covering the aircraft landing frenel lens located on the left side of the aircraft carrier which was now unusable, having been disabled by the enormous blast. Below decks metal walls that had been riveted in were now laying on the floor. The upward shock had sheared the rivets letting the walls fall where they would. On a more personal note, a sailor had taken a dump in the head, or toilet for you sand crabs, and had not flushed it. Everything that was in the toilet bowl was now on the latrine floor, mirrors were cracked over the sinks and equipment was in disarray all over the ship. On the island of the ship, which is located on the side of the flight deck, antennas were broken and had fallen down to the bridge and flight deck. The catwalk had been damaged along with some of the survival equipment, like the life rafts.

After compiling all the damage and doing some minor repair, we repeated the blast for further evaluation. When I got home and processed the film, I couldn't believe how metal, especially the catwalk rails, could bend like that. The catwalk looked like it was made of rubber during the blast, instead of iron. The rails looked like rubber garden hoses flapping in the wind. Yes, the shock trials were very interesting.

A Christmas With My Daughter

I had taken April, my teenage daughter, with me to visit my parents in Sandpoint, Idaho. We were going there for a Christmas vacation and this was her first trip to my Mom and Dad's. My parents had planned a special time for all of us. My half-brother, Willis, and his wife Ronda lived in Newman Lake, Washington, about 50 miles from Mom and Dad and would be driving up for Christmas. My sister, Paulette, her husband Terry, and their two kids, Krissy and Craig, lived in Westminster, California, and would be flying up to Spokane, Washington and renting a car to drive to Sandpoint for the reunion. Just having my family together on Christmas was the best Christmas present I could get.

April loves snow and in Maryland where we lived, though it snowed occasionally on Christmas, most of our snow came in January or February. I had talked to Mom on the phone and it was snowing then and would probably continue the whole time we'd be there. The forecast for Sandpoint called for 60 inches, and April had never seen that much snow before.

Sandpoint, Idaho in the winter is cold but dry. The snow mostly falls straight down in large storybook flakes, mainly because of the location. Sandpoint is located between Mount Casey to the north, which is 6706 feet high, and three mountainous forests: Kanikus National Forest to the east, Coeur D' Alene National Forest to the south and Colville National Forest to the north and west. The city itself is on Lake Pend Oreille in the northern part of the state, which mostly freezes over in the winter and where you can go ice fishing or ice skating all winter. Schweitzer Mountain Ski Resort can be seen, and is about five miles from Mom and Dad's house on Ella Street, in Sandpoint proper.

Skiing doesn't get much better than in Schweitzer. There is every type of ski run imaginable, all heading down towards Lake Pend Oreille, presenting a fantastic view combined with one of the best ski lodges anywhere. My parents live about two blocks from the Lake where the best trout fishing in the world can be found. Many 30 to 40 lb. Gerard Rainbow Trout and Mackinaw, or lake trout, are caught there every year. There is a city park on the lake, about one block from the house, which has every type of tree that is found in the northern part of the United States. There is an open air concert area in the park where entertainers come each year in August to hold a music festival or concert, with fireworks afterwards, for two weeks straight. It's a beautiful area and Mom and Dad have lived there for years.

When the highways of Southern California got so crowded that it took Dad hours to get to and from work, he decided to quit his good paying job and move to Sandpoint where he went to work in construction for an hourly wage. This was the only job hiring at the time. Now he says, "It's getting too crowded here and the traffic is a bit of a problem since they built that new ski resort, but it's still not like downtown Los Angeles during the rush hour." Now however, even I can see the difference in the population and traffic in the area.

Mom and Dad drove into the airport in Spokane, Washington to pick us up. As we drove back home, by the time we reached the long bridge over Pend Oreille Lake that goes into Sandpoint, the snow was coming down hard and April was all excited. There were already a couple of feet of snow on the ground and they were calling for three or four more over the next couple of days. Dad had put the Christmas tree and decorations up, and the house was lit for the season with strings of Christmas lights and wreaths of evergreens on the doors. There were electric candles in the windows and Christmas cards strung about inside the house.

By the following afternoon we had 53 inches of newly fallen snow and April was digging tunnels all throughout the backyard. I was worried that the snow was going to cave in on her, but she was having a ball, and I was keeping a worried watchful eye for cave ins.

Later we went sled riding on a long downward hill in town where four-wheel drive trucks, with chains, would take you to the top and let you out. A large white German Sheppard started chasing us and biting at my heels as I was coming down the hill on my sled with April on my back. I had to stop and chase the dog away which shortened our long sled ride and took away some of the enjoyment.

172

The snow was so deep I had to get up on the roof of both the garage and the house and shovel the snow off so the weight wouldn't break the roofs. That evening we all went on a horse-drawn sleigh-ride, and Mom made some hot buttered rum, which really hit the spot. My brother, Willis, had his snowmobile and was riding around with his wife, and I was just enjoying a wonderful Christmas with my daughter and a good time with the family. These days April goes sky diving with Sean, her husband, and I just take pictures.

This is April's half-brother Danny Dean. His father was my ex-wife's first husband and Danny lived with us for seven years after I married Patsy. Patsy has remarried since we divorced. Patsy Wood Dean Fowler Burger, quite a handle.

A Philosophical View

I am a perfectionist, but I am finding that as I age, I have begun to overlook a lot that I wouldn't have when I was younger. Does this make me a hypocrite since I've changed my mind about many areas and beliefs in life that were on the front burner when I was younger? Have I not purposed an endeavor and accomplished another task? Like being lost and being saved? Have I gained in wisdom in my old age and lived in folly throughout my youth, or have I forgotten what being young had taught me, and now I am justifying my actions with supposed experience? Is experience a better teacher than acquired knowledge? Don't you have to learn before you can do? What passion I remember long ago, and what loneliness I am living with now. Is passion forbidden me and loneliness my final reward? Is this the killing of the flesh and rebirth of the spirit that I have gained? No, I think not! Just the life I have lived - may God be pleased.

Computers

Computers have come into my life since I retired from the service. I started taking computer courses when I first realized that photography was going digital. I knew I needed to learn how to combine computers with my photography training if I was going to continue making the most of my love for photography. Besides that, the work I am doing for a navy contractor was leaning towards high speed digital photography, and I needed to either keep up or get left behind.

I am now close to having an associates degree in computer science. I need only a few more courses in English, algebra, and technical writing. I even surprised myself by maintaining a 3.5 grade point average and by getting on the dean's list. I joined the Honor Society of Charles County Community College (now the College of Southern Maryland), Phi Theta Kuppa (Beta Delta Delta chapter), and was included in the publication, The National Dean's List. As a child, the only subject I excelled in was gym. I got Ds and Fs in most other subjects except for art, and barely passed that with Cs. Being included in The National Dean's List was the first time as an adult that I had ever had my picture in a publication. However, I did raise a five legged frog one time when I was young, and Mom and I took it to the Hagerstown newspaper. They put a picture of me holding my frog on their front page; it must have been a slow week.

With a computer I can use a green screen for a picture's backdrop and then digitally place objects, people and/or things, anywhere I like: on a lake, in a forest, flying over a city, or standing by a Christmas tree. I can give it a solid background or one with a rainbow of colors. Also, I don't have to develop film or wait for it to return from the lab; and memory cards are a lot easier to handle than film, with less impact on the environment. I have two Nikon digital cameras that can cover any scene I may want to shoot and do it more efficiently, getting faster and as good or better results than with traditional film. These days everything is so automatic, all I need to do is point and shoot, which is a blessing with my deteriorating eyesight.

A computer also allows me to access the internet and shop for the best price for the equipment I need, and then order it without ever leaving the house. Additionally, through the internet and computers, I can keep up to date on new techniques in the field of photography and how to perform them, as well as have a market for my work if I intend to sell it; it even shows me suggested prices for the items. Taking computer courses has also taught me a sad but truthful fact: the more you learn, the more you realize how little you really know. And if you do learn something, it often becomes obsolete in a matter of months.

Phi Theta Kappa inductees from Charles County Community College include, front row, from left: Judith Woodburn of Mechanicsville and Damon Cruz of Accokeek. Second row, from left: Sonia Roy of Hollywood, the chapter's Community College at St. Mary's vice president; Sherri Raley of Ridge; Shawn Terwilliger of Tall Timbers; and Christine Tenney of Prince Frederick. Back row, from left: Heather Gwynn of Leonardtown; Gary Fowler of Hollywood; Joan M. Davis of Hollywood; and Earl Cross of Leonardtown.

I am the good looking one, top row between those two beautiful women.

The Let Down

It was near Christmas time and I was visiting my mom and my step-dad in Sandpoint, Idaho. I only visit them every other year because of the expense, but I look forward to each visit. It is about three thousand and twenty- five miles from my house in Hollywood, Maryland to Sandpoint, Idaho. My sister, Paulette, who lives in Ontario, California and my half-brother, Willis and his wife Rhonda, who live in Newman Lake, Washington and I, try to get together whenever we can. Our family has always been separated for one reason or another. I joined the Air Force, then Mom and Dad moved to Idaho, and Paulette stayed in California after Mom and Dad moved away. Even Willis moved out of the house when he got married. He now lives in Newman Lake, Washington, which is only fifty miles from Sandpoint, Idaho, but still a good distance for a working family to visit.

Only Willis has had the advantage of being raised by both his mother and father. Paulette and my step-sister, Carolina, Willis's half-sister from his Dad's first marriage, and I, had only a mother or grandparent to raise us. Willis's only disadvantage in life was his first marriage which didn't work out; even then, he has three fine sons, Chris, Mat, and Erin, to his credit, and he married a wonderful woman the second time around, named Ronda. She is younger them Willis and smart as a whip, everyone loves Ronda. I call Willis my baby brother because of our age difference, me being the oldest, but he is six feet four inches tall and inherited Dad's ability to invent, fix, and/or repair just about anything. He is also a hard worker and a perfectionist like Dad, and this particular year he showed me he is also one hell of a man.

Willis loves to go snowmobiling and has souped up his snowmobile for racing. He had also just bought his wife a new snowmobile. She hadn't even ridden on it yet when Mom suggested, while I was up visiting, that Willis take me up on the mountain and we go snowmobiling together. Willis was just dying to show off his snowmobiles and wanted to take me on top of a very high mountain with a lake on top, which was frozen, so we could open up the snowmobiles and see what they would do. I had never been snowmobiling before, but I am adventuresome and it sounded like fun to me. We took the snowmobiles on a trailer by truck as far up the mountain as we could and then unloaded the trailer, thus beginning our adventure. Following the trail as far as we could by snowmobile, we came upon about three feet of freshly fallen snow. Willis said that if we hugged the side of the mountain we would be okay, and that I should just follow him. He led the way, trying to make a trail along the side of this mountain with a thirty degree pitch and I followed behind. We were going slowly when I hit a bump, and to this day I don't know what it was, but it threw me off the snowmobile. The snowmobile just kept on going with me sitting in the snow watching it. It wasn't going fast, just idling along, and though I got up, in three feet of snow I couldn't run fast enough to catch it. It just turned downhill and kept on going. The farther it went, the more the slight of the mountain and the greater the pitch. Finally it went over a hill and out of sight. I envisioned the snowmobile in pieces at the bottom of a mountainous ravine.

About that time Willis looked back and saw what had happened, his wife's new snowmobile going down the mountain and out of sight with me standing in the snow watching it. I may have been his big brother, but at that time I felt pretty small. He parked his snowmobile and started walking down the mountain, following the trail of the runaway snowmobile. He turned and hollered, "Stay here, I'll be right back." I watched not only the snowmobile go over the hill and out of sight, but then my baby brother went over the hill and out of sight. I walked down to where the hill started its quick descent, trying to see, but I saw no snowmobile and no brother. I started back to where he had parked his snowmobile, and I was out of breath when I got there. Smoking for forty years had taken its toll on my body and I was no longer able to do the things I remember doing when I was younger. Walking up hill in three feet of snow was one

180

of those things. I wasn't sure how far Willis would have to go to retrieve the snowmobile, or even if he could, and all I could do was wait, which seemed like a very long time. I sat on his snowmobile, pulled out a cigarette, and started thinking about what had happened. The mountain view was not only beautiful, but quiet except for the sharp brisk wind shaping the powdered snow that had fallen. Then it came to me that I was alone on the top of a mountain with grizzly bears, mountain lions, wolves, and whatever else might be looking for lunch.

As I was trying my best not to get anxious, I heard in the distance the sound of an engine. Suddenly, there was Willis going back and forth, coming up the side of the mountain. Apparently the snowmobile had come to rest on a stump and tree, partially breaking only the left front rudder. Willis had managed to retrieve and drive it back up the mountain. I could tell he wasn't a happy camper and our snowmobiling adventure was over. Back to the truck and home we went not talking too much. I offered to pay for the damage, but Willis being a perfectionist, saw only damaged property now that needed to be replaced.

Before I left for home I gave him a signed blank check to use as he wanted. Mom talked to him later and he returned my check, and I think Mom paid the tab. But Willis did show me that day that he was one hell of a man, and I have always been sorry that his big brother let him down.

Art 1100

I had always wanted to be able to draw a portrait. I would watch others do it and they made it seem so easy. So I decided to take a class in basic drawing. I was already taking some college courses but they were for computer training and weren't art oriented. I signed up for basic drawing 1, ART 1100. Halfway through the course we had live nude models come into class. I did not expect to be in a class with nude models and really didn't know how to act. But our teacher, Mrs. Carrie Fickes, handled the class very professionally and everything went well. Nothing came up that shouldn't have. They weren't that attractive anyway. And I did learn how to draw a portrait, but a Picasso I am not.

Original picture

Drawing I did after class

Drawing I did in class

Original picture

Trick or Treat

       I noticed that I was getting very tired easily. Cutting grass or just walking a short distance, I would get out of breath. Sometimes both of my wrists would have a burning sensation in them, and that's when I knew something wasn't right, so I went to see my regular physician, Dr. Saasa, in the New Bean Medical Center. He made an appointment for me to have a stress test at the end of the month with Doctor A. K. Shaw, who was also in the New Bean Medical Center, in Hollywood, Maryland.

       As the month went by, and as long as I didn't overdo anything, everything seemed okay. At work though, I had trouble. Each morning we had to check out our theodolite tracking instrument and kinetic tracking mount to make sure they were operational, and to do this I had to climb two flights of stairs. I was always huffing and puffing when I reached the top, so I learned to take my time and not rush, but I still wondered what was really wrong.

       Finally, October 31, 2003, rolled around—it came on a Friday that year—and I went for my appointment with Doctor Shaw. I felt fine, and like in all doctors' offices, I was put on hold as soon as I walked in the door and checked at the desk. In my 61 years I don't believe I had ever seen a doctor exactly at my appointment time. It was Halloween, kids were out trick or treating, and I wanted to get this stress test over with so I could go home and see any trick or treaters that may come to my door.

Patience is a virtue, and I finally got to go in and get on the treadmill. They hooked me up to wires to monitor my heart, and then put me on the treadmill and told me to start walking. They wanted to raise my heart rate to see if there were any abnormalities. I got tired in a short amount of time, which was strange, but I guessed it was nothing to worry about because the doctor told the nurses to give me an injection to speed up my heart rate so they could monitor it while I was on the treadmill.

The doctor then started to look over the data that had already been taken during my short walk on the treadmill. The nurses started hooking me up with an I.V. so they could give me the shot, but suddenly Doctor Shaw said, "We need to get you to the hospital." When I heard that, I know my heart started to move faster. It scared me, and I didn't know what to do at that time. The doctor told the nurse to call an ambulance. He then told me he was transporting me to Saint Mary's Hospital, and then to Washington Central in the morning. He said my EKG test showed some abnormalities, and that I needed further tests at the hospital to see where the blockages in my heart were. I didn't know what to say except that I needed to call my daughter, and so they let me use the phone while I waited on the ambulance.

I got a hold of my daughter, April, who lived in Baltimore, Maryland, and told her what was going on. I told her where I had parked the truck so she could pick it up and take it home. I told her she needed to contact Rose, my fiancée, in Martinsburg, West Virginia, and my sister Paulette, who is a doctor and lives in Yorba Linda, California at that time. I also told her that Pastor

Conner of Patuxent Baptist Church should be contacted, as well as the folks where I work. My mind was going a hundred miles per hour. I think I told April not to worry, but I am not sure.

I do know that I was very anxious, which Doctor Shaw sensed, and he and the nurses came over to reassure me. The ambulance showed up and they placed me on a table with wheels. I was taken to the hospital and given a room by myself. I was thinking, what a difference a day makes. I went to work that morning, and now I was in the hospital. April and her husband, Sean, came for a short visit that night. I stayed in Saint Mary's Hospital until Saturday afternoon, when they then took me by ambulance to Washington Central Hospital.

They don't operate on Sundays, so I was prepared for an exploratory operation for Monday morning; nice way to start a week. I still was very anxious, but the surgeon had a good bedside manner, and he put me somewhat at ease. Also the Twenty-third Psalm came to mind, "Even though I walk through the valley of the shadow of death, I fear no evil, for thou art with me." I felt the peace that the bible says passes all understanding, and that put me completely at ease.

Rose, my fiancée, April and Sean, and Pastor Conner and his wife Lori, came and visited me Sunday evening. The surgeon who was going to perform the exploratory operation also came to see me. After that, the nurse gave me a suppository, which got things moving, and I went to sleep. I was awakened in the early morning and taken to a preparation room where many other people were also being prepared for surgery. The interesting thing about this room was that it was about forty feet long, and one whole wall was nothing but beautiful pictures. They were all pictures of outdoor scenery on glass, from ceiling to floor, and the wall was lit from behind by a soft light, giving the effect of the room being in the pictures. I guess it was supposed to calm the patients before surgery. Being a photographer, I was quite impressed, and could picture a home done that same way.

I told the nurse that I was allergic to pain and didn't care to see any of the operation, which I am sure he had heard a thousand times before. The next thing I remember is waking up and the surgeon telling me, with his pleasing bedside manner, that I needed a quintuple bypass. Then another doctor, who was in charge of the anesthesia part of this operation, wanted to look into my mouth to see if there were any obstructions to be encountered. Still recalling Psalm Twenty-three, I said, okay to the surgery. I knew I was saved by accepting my Lord Jesus Christ's work on the cross, and if this was my time to go, I was ready.

That was Monday, and Rose, April and Sean visited me that night. What April didn't tell me, and probably didn't know, was they had gotten a ticket in my car, coming to see me. I didn't find out until I got home and received a notice from the District of Columbia. They sent me a photograph of my license plate on the rear of my Buick and noted the speed it was going, saying I owed Washington D.C., one hundred dollars for speeding.

My sister, from California, called telling me she had to call Mom and Dad, which I didn't think was a good idea because of their age. I had told my daughter to tell her that when she contacted Paulette, but left the decision up to my sister whether to tell them or not. Mom and Dad then gave me a call from Idaho, letting me know everything was going to be alright. I received some calls from Bill Dodge, Buddy Long, and Ed Bell at work, wishing me well. And then I was given some pills and out I went until after the operation.

I woke up feeling very weak with numbness in my chest. I had a tube in my nose and a clamp on a wire connected to my finger, as well as what felt like a board on my side and tubes in my upper stomach. But at least I was awake, and they had put me by a window in a room with another person. Every half hour or so they came in and drew some blood. After a while I figured out who could draw blood and who couldn't, a hard way to learn. The day was Tuesday, I was still alive, and the operation seemed to have gone well.

The older man in the room with me didn't seem to be doing as well as me so I felt fortunate. He had nine bypasses—I didn't know you could have that many--plus they had installed a pacemaker in him. Rose and I met his wife later that week and she seemed to be a really nice person; we felt sorry for her and her husband.

Each day I got stronger and was able to do more and more for myself, like going to the bathroom and taking a bath. I guess the worst thing about being in the hospital was the food. It all tasted like wet cardboard, and the only thing I even remotely liked were the sherbet ice creams and juices: cranberry and raspberry mixed, or apple and cranberry. Even the plain salad, which was mostly lettuce, tasted bland.

188

They would have let me go Friday, but I stayed until Saturday morning. Rose took time off of work to stay with me until I could cook and do things for myself. I was off work and on disability for about six months. My disability insurance covered the whole time, so money wasn't a problem. Rose came down on the weekends and any other time she could, to look after me.

We are no longer together and I believe the Lord brought her into my life just to take care of me during this time of sickness. We met not too long before this happened, and we split up not long after I got back on my feet after the operation. We both knew marriage wasn't for us. She gave me back my engagement ring and left for her home in West Virginia. I never saw or heard from her again. The more I think about this the more I am persuaded that she was sent by God to take care of me. I am truly thankful for her.

The operation cost about a quarter of a million dollars, and thank God again I had the insurance, and the time in the service for medical coverage for this expense.

Thanks To Dear Old Dad

  My mother was beaten, abandoned, and left to raise two small children. My sister, Paulette, and I were born in Martinsburg, West Virginia, and we had a brother, Donnie, but he died of pneumonia when he was just a baby. They didn't have the medicines then that they have today, and pneumonia was deadly. Mother raised us after moving to Hagerstown, Maryland. She operated a beauty salon, and was quite popular as a beautician and hair stylist. When Donnie passed away, Mom bought a gravesite with four plots on it. She never received a cent from my biological father. I remember coming home on leave from the Air Force one time and my biological dad had come to Hagerstown then to meet with Paulette and me. Paulette came up and told me he was downstairs, and that he would like to meet me. I told her to tell him that he wasn't there when I needed him and that I didn't need him now. I did this for two reasons, out of respect for my mother, and because I was angry that he hadn't been there when I needed a father for guidance. Right or wrong, that was how I felt. He didn't exist as far as I was concerned.

Over the years my mother remarried and moved to Idaho. She gave the grave plots to me since I was the oldest child in the family and I still lived on the East Coast. Mom and my step-dad bought two other grave plots in Idaho for themselves.

My sister continued seeing my biological dad until one Thanksgiving when he passed away while she was visiting him. He left everything to Skippy, one of his sons by another marriage, but he had lived in Florida and Skippy lived in West Virginia. Skippy didn't want to come down for the funeral because he didn't have anything to claim and money was tight for him. Sis, living in California, was left holding the ashes and an old car. She had missed her flight (and could not get another in time for work) because she stayed with Dad at the hospital and had his remains cremated. She ended up driving the car back to California.

Now the plot thickens. Skippy, dear old Dad's beneficiary, was entitled to the car. But, since the car was in California and Skippy was in West Virginia, and since Sis had been left with the ashes, she contacted Skippy to get a title for the car so she could get it registered. The car was worth a little over a thousand dollars. But Skippy wanted the ashes because he said dear old Dad had told him he wanted his ashes spread over the race track in Charlestown, West Virginia. Sis never did get the title for the car, and the longer she waited, the angrier she got. The ashes remained as they were, stored in Paulette's garage for many years. Meanwhile, I had a mad brother and a madder sister, thanks to dear old Dad, a man I never knew. I talked to Mom about it and she convinced Sis to bring the ashes to West Virginia and have them spread over the Fowler gravesites near the plot where my brother Donnie is buried. I wanted to make peace between my sister Paulette, and my half-brother Skippy, so I suggested that he (dear old Dad) be placed in one of the plots given to me by Mom. This seemed to make everyone happy, not doing what Skippy wanted and not doing what Paulette wanted, but also not doing what Mom wanted. So I deeded two plots to Sis, and gave her the money to bury dear old Dad because she didn't have the money. Paulette's wish was to be cremated and buried with me when the time came. So the secret I must keep now is to never tell Mom who is buried in her plots. Thanks to dear old Dad.

This is my biological father, Howard Earl Fowler. People who knew him before he passed away called him "Mac." I never knew him except for an Easter egg hunt when I was very little. And then he was only a man in a trench coat.

The Last Word

It was my birthday, August 18th, and I was at my mother's house in Idaho. She had told me to come up then so she, Dad, and I could spend some time together without the rest of the kids. Mom was 84 and Dad was 82. Having too many people around at their age was like riding a subway car during the morning rush hour. Mom's eyes were getting bad, she couldn't see well even with glasses, and Dad's hearing was almost gone. He could hear some tones but others just didn't register, and a hearing aid just whistled in his ears. All day long, Mom would ask Dad a question and he wouldn't answer, so eventually, she would have to shout to get his attention. Even then I think he was reading her lips.

All her life, Mom loved pretty things, especially flowers. She used to make flower arrangements for the church every Sunday. Most of the flowers came from her backyard, but just sometimes she would buy plastic flowers to mix with her own. People just loved her arrangements, but at her age she slowly had to give up things that gave her life meaning. The loss of eyesight, especially for a creative person who loves a colorful world, is a cruel thing only the devil could render.

Dad has two interests. He loves cigars, which he smokes outside, and I always brought him the best I could find because he would never buy them for himself.

He also enjoys raising pure white pigeons. To keep
the numbers down, he would kill or sell any that weren't
white. He had twelve this particular year, and four eggs. I
loved to watch them flying in the skies over Sandpoint, Idaho.
They would fly together in formation and spiral down towards
earth. Dad said sometimes one or two of them would not recover
from their dives and hit the ground. I never saw that happen, but
I did see them come very close to the ground.

Dad always had a pellet rifle ready inside the garage
for hawks that went after his pigeons. He lost one or two a year
to this bird of prey. Dad would sit on the back porch in the
evenings smoking a cigar, and the pigeons would come down and
eat the ashes as they dropped off the cigar he was smoking.
The three of us were sitting on the back porch and I
was trying to show off my new digital camera. Dad is a
perfectionist and not an artistic individual, so when I showed

him the digital picture of his birds, he pointed out that the year was 2005, not 2004. I decided he should have the last word. After all, "father knows best," and the date at the bottom of the picture did read   08 14 2004.

I will return again next year to Idaho because life is short and time waits for no man. By then I should have the date right on the camera even, so Dad will have the last word.

My Favorite Song

A song I will never forget, and one I am reminded of each year, is the Happy Birthday song. This song is always sung during times filled with laughter, presents, and excitement. There is usually a cake with candles to blow out, a wish and a prayer you can blow them out, the excitement of your friends, and your own embarrassment as everyone sings happy birthday to you. The moment is filled with wonder and the hope of what will come next, what kind of cake you'll have, and what presents everyone got for you. This is truly my favorite song. Oh yes! don't forget the ice cream. ☺

A Terrific View

    Not many people get to start their day with a view like this, but I have been fortunate enough to do just that.

    In October, 1981, I retired from the Air Force and started working for a contractor named Dyn-a-Electron. The name eventually changed to DynCorp, and they are now part of Computer Science Corporation (CSC). They are contracted by the Navy to provide technical support for Patuxent Naval Air Base in Maryland, on the shores of the Chesapeake Bay.

    I have been working there for 25 years as an engineering technician, and I never get tired of seeing the picturesque view of the

Chesapeake Bay in the morning. I see bald eagles, osprey, storks, seagulls, ducks, swans, and many other birds. The waters are alive with schools of fish, otters, skates, jellyfish, and many other things you just don't find in your average back yard.

We surely have a treasure in the Chesapeake Bay. I hope we don't lose it for our kids. Each year the harvest of fish, crabs, and oysters becomes less than the year before, and the consuming population becomes more. Are we out growing this environment? Or will our technology save us? Me, I look for the Lord Jesus Christ to come; He has already saved us if we let Him.

Me

It is time to reflect on what might have been, what is going on now, and what will take place in the future. Looking back I see things that I wish I had done, things that I regret doing, and things I am glad that I had the good sense to do.

Saving the best for last, I will start with the things I wish I had done, like studying harder in school. I know that I was handicapped all my life by not learning to read and spell better. Of course there were reasons for it, but I still feel I should have tried harder to overcome my insecurity and speech impediment.

Something else I regret is not finding a companion in this lifetime to share the joys and sorrows I have been through. I feel there must be a character flaw in my makeup for me to have loved twice and lost both loves. There are things that happened in both relationships that were my fault, but there are always two sides to a story and it's the ending that history always remembers and regrets.

Patting myself on the back, I can only recall my salvation experience on Guam, putting that on the top of the list. Of course there is also my daughter who I love and get prouder of every day. Given my circumstances, I am glad I stayed in the service, but I believe it was more from insecurity than anything else. I do believe God has watched over my life, guiding me and bringing me back onto a straighter path whenever I went astray.

Now, in the Fall of my life, I find myself retired from the Air Force after 22 years, which earns me a small income. I've worked for a Navy contractor for 25 years, which has helped provide me with a 401k balance and job security. I have a nice house, a beautiful daughter and son-in-law, I am active in a church, and people seem to like me. However, I am lonely at times, and yet glad I am alone at times. My immediate family is not near. My sister, Paulette, is in California, my half-brother, Willis, is in Washington State, my mom and dad are in Idaho, and my half-brother, Skippy, and step-sister, Carolyn, are in Martinsburg, West Virginia. But I have no family members near me in Southern Maryland. Even my daughter, April, lives in Baltimore, Maryland with her husband Sean, and I have no grandkids yet to visit or play with and spoil. I am a Past Master of the Masonic Lodge, and a member of the Moose Lodge, the VFW, and the American Legion, none of which I have visited lately because of being active in the church. The church doesn't like drinking or secret organizations, and I don't want people to gossip. Personally though, I don't see anything wrong with either, as long as drinking is done in moderation or for medicinal purposes; and organizations that promote peace, brotherly love and stand for the betterment of mankind or self improvement are needed in this violent world we live in.

Looking ahead, I see social security and retirement maybe when I am sixty-five years old, and perhaps a cruise or two, though to where I am not sure. As I look around me I see a fast approaching rapture of the church as referred to in the Bible. I see a generation of people growing up that I never knew who are smart but who are not adding wisdom to their learning. I see brother against brother, and hatred increasing, motivated by selfishness. I see a world that I feel sorry for and will be glad to leave when the Lord comes for me, for God is love and without God I would rather be gone.

My prayer is for the living, that they may prefer love over hatred, and may God look after our children as He has looked after me. Amen.

This is my house in Hollywood, Maryland, where I planted an apple tree and watched it grow.

My Two Mile Walk

     My office sits on the bank of the Chesapeake Bay. From there I track aircraft and other aerospace vehicles—balloons, rockets, etc. — for the military to evaluate and improve upon. On days when things are slack, I try to get my exercise by taking a two mile walk. I start by putting a lock on the office door, and then again on the gate that leads into my station's compound, which has a fence all the way around it for security reasons.

     The station is located at the end of a long narrow road on the Chesapeake Bay. There are targets set in the middle of the water so aircraft can practice shooting or dropping laser-guided missiles and bombs. From the main road to the station is about one mile, so I walk from the station to the main road and back, which usually takes me 30 minutes. There is normally no traffic, and only virgin forest on both sides of the asphalt road leading to the station. There are a few homes on this road, but I hardly ever see anyone. As a matter of fact, I see more wildlife than anything else.

One of the first things I notice when starting my walk are the "Private Property" signs posted along both sides of the road by people trying to claim and protect their property from "the good, the bad, and the ugly," declaring their legal right to this solitude provided by Mother Nature. There are still many beer cans, plastic bags, cups and other trash that people so readily discard, rather than holding on to them and putting them in a garbage can as good neighbors should. Their reasoning is: "why bother, it's not my property."

The first house I come upon is to my right, an older building constructed in the late 40s or early 50s. It has been restored with bright yellow vinyl siding and has a new brown shingle roof, reminding me of Hansel and Gretel's cottage, being set deep into the woods as it was. Only, I don't remember a swimming pool in the fairy tale. The pool, like the house, is also older, and set above ground with a contemporary look about it. It must be for the children in that family. Although, with cleaning out leaves, tree branches, bugs, snakes, and frogs, not to mention the cost of chemicals, you could hardly justify it for the kids. A rope hanging from a tree that swung out into the creek is all we ever had when I was a boy. The creek carried the leaves and branches away, and the water wasn't polluted, so no need for chemicals; and when we dropped off the end of the rope, the bugs, snakes and frogs got out of the way. Things seemed to take care of themselves. I didn't have much, but I really didn't need much, and I was thankful for what I did have.

Walking past this gingerbread house, I begin to notice the tall majestic trees towering over the narrow lane, the clouds appearing to settle in their branches, and the sounds of insects welcoming me to their environment. The woods grow deep and mysterious as I continue my walk. The vines grow up the trees, strangling the very host that takes them to the sunlight they seek. Yet, the mighty oaks pay little attention to these invaders of their space, and continue to grow higher. Their branches look like veins feeding the clouds that nestle in them. These are woods that Robert Frost might have been tempted to enter. But today they are mine. I quicken my steps and breathe the moist air deep into my lungs as if it has magical powers to make me young again.

After what seems like only a short while, I come to a curve in the road that turns back on itself, making an "s" shape. Another house to my left and on a slight incline comes into view. The two Huskies that normally announce my arrival from behind the fenced yard must still be in the house. I hear only the birds calling from the woods, making the sounds of the insects seem faint; or maybe just changing the melody of the woodland orchestra, of which Mother Nature has so many rhythmic sequences.

I walk past the house, and there is a bamboo forest to my left. The tops reach nearly twenty feet high, and the base of each plant is two to three inches in diameter. What a fortress that would make if only I was a kid again! I continue on, still listening to the birds and wondering if they are announcing my arrival or just calling to their

204

mates. Perhaps there is danger in the area, a snake invading their nest, or another predator stealing their eggs. Or maybe it's just a song God gave them to sing. It seems to go well with the insects' accompaniment.

Five more minutes and I come to another house with a driveway leading up to it and a sign that reads, "Beware Moose Crossing." I wonder what the people are like that live there. The yard is carefully manicured with many flowers and bushes, and I notice an American flag on a new mailbox—probably for Hurricane Katrina's victims. The new mailbox was put up after someone hit the old one with a baseball bat while driving by. This world is getting so destructive. I wonder if the kids really know right from wrong, or if they are just crying out for attention.

I leave this house behind and move on up the road. A squirrel runs across the road ahead of me. He jumps into the tall grass on the side of the road. Not being able to see over the grass, he hops like a rabbit while making his way to the trees. Soon he disappears behind a large pine tree. I look into the forest and think about how many other animals are watching me and waiting for me to pass by so they can continue on with their lives, hunting and being hunted, and searching for food for the oncoming winter.

I see the main road now. Halfway point, a place to begin my downhill treck back to the Chesapeake Bay and my work site. Walking slowly but steadily uphill to the main road provided a good workout, but going downhill is a good way to return. Reaching the halfway point, I cross the road and head back. Cars pass on the main road every minute or so in a hurry to get where they are going, for whatever reason.

Half a block down the forest road two fawns skip by, their heads and tails held high, as if to snub the main highway they are moving away from. Once inside the forest they stop and look back as if to see if anyone noticed them, then they start to feed on the forest floor. They seem not to notice me as I walk by, still marveling at the sight of them. I begin to hear the cadence of my own footsteps again, sounding like someone chewing on hard cereal, with each step becoming louder than the last.

The electric and telephone lines on the poles along the side of the road have been cleared of all branches and limbs, with the tops cut out of the trees as they become higher. Extended limbs have been removed already from higher trees, giving the forest a manmade look of neatness, ensuring our survival, but being unforgiving to Mother Nature's field of expertise. The neatness soon becomes a deposit for plastic forks and lids and the "king of beer" cans.

The clouds have now moved deeper into the trees, and a mist mixes with the forest. The solitude this provides me is a most welcomed change from the televisions, telephones, cars, airplanes, and new technology of this generation. The main road no longer interrupts the woodland music in my ears. Only the birds, insects and frogs in a stream to my left, now have my attention. My feet still chew up the road beneath me, as if they too are hungry for the solitude about them. But in the end, they will be on my desk taking a rest as I wait for the clock to reach four p.m.

A lot more escaped my attention on that two mile walk, but there will always be tomorrow. I look out on the Bay at the pylons with seagulls on them, each seeming to have their own space, and I wonder what our offspring will see, hear, and have tomorrow.

Not My Will

A different path will make you either early or late. I have spent a lifetime trying to keep an open mind to the world around me, and I've found there are no set answers except what is written in the Bible. And even then, I do not always make the right decisions, and I arrive either early or late depending on the path I choose.

As a youth I searched for pleasure and fulfillment, and with temperateness I found both, and yet I gained neither. For it was like air, one breath at a time, but never a reservoir that lasts. Now that I am aging, in hindsight I see my mistakes, looking back as though through a tunnel, thinking I could have done better. But was not that my thinking or intention in the past? The Bible tells me there is a time for all things, but only the will of God will prevail.

So what path must I take but that which Love has put before me; all else is foolishness. I give thanks to be able to choose, but I choose not my will, for it is a will that would take a different path, and I do not wish to be either early or late on the path towards eternity.

Stained Glass

Stained glass is one of my hobbies and these are just a few of the hundreds of pieces I have made.

I made these for our visiting Missionaries.

This was the first one I made for Patuxent Baptist Church.

This one is 4 feet high and 8 feet long and is mounted inside Patuxent Baptist Church's new building.

My favorite!

     This is the only one I kept for myself out of the hundreds of pieces I made. It reminds me of St. Mary's County.

I close this book with John 3:16 from the Bible.
For God so loved the world that he gave his only Son,
that whoever believes in him should not perish but have
eternal life.
So today is only the beginning for me, what about you?

Printed in the United States
By Bookmasters